I0558683

# PHILIP "SHARP SKILLS" JACOBS

IS

# GLADIATOR

FEATURING

*Modern Parables for Building
Resilience and Mental Toughness*

PUBLISHED BY

**Rebel Firm Books, Spanaway, WA**

# PHILIP "SHARP SKILLS" JACOBS

# GLADIATOR

To Phil Jr. and Jonathan. I'm proud of the strong and solid young men you are and who you are becoming.

You yourself have to be tough because the biggest battle that you have is with yourself. What you say to me when you tell me what I can and can't do will not affect me or discourage me unless I allow it to. If you want to get to your dreams and accomplish your goals, you have to be able to deal with yourself. Stay positive and don't talk to yourself in a negative way. Continue to stay on your path. Continue to get better, and better, and better. But you can't do that without being inwardly tough with yourself.

— Kobe Bryant

# GLADIATOR

CHAPTER

ONE

# DIVORCE

**B**rian sat on his hotel room bed with menacing butterflies fluttering through his stomach. It was an unwanted sensation he couldn't shake since his wife, Debra, whom he'd been married to for ten years, told him she wanted a divorce two weeks earlier. That was something he never expected to happen. He and Debra virtually grew up together in their marriage, having gotten married in their early twenties. Much of Brian's personal identity was wrapped up in being a husband and he was having a painfully difficult time. He kept disassociating from his current reality of being a single man with his not-so-distant past of being married.

The thing that made his new reality real to him was the fact that he was now living in a hotel room, a three-star rated hotel room, at best, with a kitchenette. He had moved out of the family home when he found out Debra was having an affair with one of her co-workers, whom she referred to as her "brother from another mother."

"Some brother alright, laying the pipe in her every chance he got..." Brian muttered to himself.

He knew if he stayed in the home he and Debra bought together, he would end up doing a life sentence in prison. He couldn't bear the thought of his now four-year-old son, Isaiah, growing up without his dad. On top of the divorce, Brian had a new and demanding position at work which required him to show up at his best everyday. And, the temporary custody schedule that was in place had Isaiah staying with him three to four days out of the week. Isaiah was the definition of a four-year-old boy. He was full of energy. Brian was doing his best to engage with Isaiah the way he needed it, taking him to the park and other activities as often as he could. But there were only so many pillow fights and jumping on the bed they could do before it started getting old. The hotel made things feel cramped for the both of them. Isaiah kept asking questions about why they couldn't just go back home. Plus the pick and drop off schedule was wearing both Brian and Isaiah thin, with Isaiah having to sit through a 35-minute commute back to the hotel.

Dealing with the stressors of the divorce, his new gig, and single fatherhood all left Brian beyond exhausted. To cope, he resorted to heavy drinking, excessive eating, and porn consumption. When he looked in the mirror, he didn't even recognize the man he was anymore. He felt like a zombie, even when he played with his son. Even worse, as much as he loved his precious Isaiah, it was draining to raise him during this time period. He often felt like a bad father because he wasn't as present as he used to be. And boy, did Isaiah remind him of it. Isaiah was an incredibly intelligent and empathetic child.

"Daddy, daddy, put your phone away," Isaiah would often say as Brian scrolled the endless sea of social media nothingness.

Brian would put his phone away for a brief moment to appease his son, but then would quickly reach for it again after a few minutes, out of habit. It got to the point that Isaiah would just start playing by himself. Brian was often heavily distracted and still somewhat obsessed with his ex-wife. He thought about who her lover or lovers might be.

"That bitch!" he sometimes yelled out when he was alone and Isaiah was out of the house. Brian had nightmares about Debra moving on with her life and how amazing her life was without him. He stalked her social media profile and she definitely made it look like she was living her best life. She posted sexy pictures of herself with captions that suggested she was "back to her old self." Brian broke into cold sweats in the middle of the night as he tossed and turned thinking about it. He had lost sight of how horrible his marriage was while he was in it. All he could think of was the good times. This is common for people who get dumped. "Rejection breeds obsession," as Coach Corey Wayne often says.

Brian realized the toll the relationship had taken on him was immense. He was now alienated from most of his family and friends. He couldn't remember the last time he talked to his mother or father. Debra often remarked how she felt she played second fiddle to Brian's family, and because of that, he distanced himself from them to assuage her feelings. He didn't realize it at the time, but he'd given up a core part of who he was by doing this. And, Debra lost more and more respect for him as he yielded to her wishes. He thought he was just being a good husband. The truth is, many women are drawn to men who lead with confidence and stand firmly in their values. When a man consistently wavers or loses his sense of direction, it can diminish the sense of security and attraction in the relationship. Tears of anger and frustration rolled down Brian's cheeks as he thought about all this. He looked at his son, sleeping peacefully in the full-size bed they shared in his hotel room. Brian was tired and restless at the same time. He felt like everything he had worked so hard for had been snatched away from him in an instant. His family home, his family members, his reputation in the community, his entire life! Dismayed, he went to the bathroom where he demonstrated his hopelessness by masturbating to his favorite porn star on Twitter. Then he quietly drank himself to sleep on the opposite end of the hotel room from his son.

The next day, after Brian dropped Isaiah off at daycare, he went for a drive through his old neighborhood. He observed how the houses and community hadn't changed much since he had grown up and moved away. Suddenly, an unusual but enticing thought took center stage in his mind. *What if I was no longer here*? Brian had never been suicidal before, so he was startled this thought popped up inside him. But the exit opportunity it provided for him was something he couldn't help but further mentally pursue. He began to plan scenarios out: he had a two million dollar life insurance policy that Isaiah would get if he passed away along with some other assets that Brian had been building.

*Then maybe Isaiah wouldn't see the shell of a man his father has become,* he thought to himself. *He'll remember me as someone who left him with a significant amount of money that he could pursue his dreams with and build a life he loves.*

This idea became intoxicating to Brian as he thought about his son doing all the things he couldn't, or that he thought he couldn't. Traveling, dating all sorts of beautiful women, buying an expensive home, driving luxury cars...

"My son will be set!" he said aloud to himself while driving.

But as soon as Brian began to drift deeper into this twisted daydream, another thought crept in. He saw how misguided Isaiah would be without the influence of his father in his life. Isaiah might end up in prison, or on drugs, or seek validation from the streets. Brian saw Isaiah at some point even contemplating suicide and becoming a much more violent version of himself. This was enough to get Brian to come to his senses. That, along with the black SUV behind him that kept honking to get his attention because the light was now green.

Brian waived apologetically to the driver behind him and headed back toward the hotel so he could start his work day. The day was dreary and gray, not unusual for the fall in the Pacific Northwest. When Brian got back to his hotel room, he was not motivated to work even though he had a day full of meetings.

"Fuck..." he said.

He felt trapped and hopeless. Here he was making more money than he ever had, with a great job, but he could not enjoy it because of how wounded his heart was. He was extremely broken and he knew it. He was perplexed about how things could be going so right in one area of his life and horribly wrong in another. He felt like a rudder without a ship and all he could see in his future was deep, pitch black darkness. After about twenty minutes of sitting and staring at the ceiling, he made a cup of nasty coffee, which was all the hotel had to offer, and he plopped down on the uncomfortable faux leather swivel chair in front of his computer so he could hop onto his first virtual meeting of the day.

Just as he was getting ready to click the link for his meeting, he yelled out loud from all the pain of his inner turmoil. And then he just kept yelling at the top of his lungs. He yelled so loud he surprised even himself. Normally, he was a very reserved, even-keel type of guy, but his soul was crying out. After he belted out the last yell he could muster, he sent his assistant a text message asking her to cancel all his meetings for the day. He couldn't bring himself to plow forward any longer. He was at his wits end and he was afraid because he had never been here before, emotionally or mentally. He grabbed the bottle of whiskey on the kitchenette counter and took a big guzzle from it until he drank about half of the liquor inside. He plopped onto the bed and fell asleep.

*Buzz, Buzz, Buzz.*

Brian's phone was vibrating back-to-back from several missed calls from his soon to be ex-wife. He awoke from his drunken sleep.

"Hel... hello?" he stammered.

"You no good son of a bitch, guess what I'm doing?" fired Debra.

Brian was still coming to. "What, what's your problem?"

"I picked up our son from daycare, an hour after he was supposed to be picked up by his no good father."

Brian looked over at the alarm clock and saw that it was 6:00 p.m. He had slept the entire day away. In a surge of adrenaline, he jumped up to get ready to run out the door.

"Oh shit, I'm sorry babe, I mean Deb. I was exhausted today and overslept."

"It's okay," Debra retorted sarcastically. "I picked him up since the daycare couldn't get a hold of you. Super mom to the rescue again. Brian, you really need to get your shit together. And until you do, I think it's best that Isaiah lives with me full time."

Brian couldn't believe what he was hearing. He knew he was a good dad, he had just made a mistake due to all the pressure he was under. But he couldn't form any words to respond at that moment.

He was shocked that she was suggesting such a thing. He was seeing a new level of cruelty from her that he didn't know she was capable of.

"Helloooo? Are you there? Earth to Brian..."

"Yeah, yeah, I'm here. I'm just, you know... you caught me off guard with that. No, Isaiah needs both of us in his life. I don't think that's a good idea. Look, I'm sorry I inconvenienced you by having to pick up Isaiah today. Being that this is the only time this has happened, I think I deserve some grace. I would offer you the same. I mean, it's not like the process of a divorce is easy on any of us. I'm gonna come pick him up from you right now, okay."

"He's asleep and I don't want to disturb him. Brian, I think this is for the best. Isaiah needs a stable routine and all of this going back and forth really isn't good for him at this age."

"Then why not let him live with me? I'm actually moving into my new place two weeks from now. I've signed the lease and they are waiting for the old tenant to move out before they get the apartment ready for me. I've already got furniture in storage, including stuff for Iasiah's room."

Debra had underestimated Brian throughout their entire marriage. Brian knew she didn't think he could stand on his own two feet without her. He also knew she had made up her mind and was going to try to force him to go along with her plan.

"An apartment?" she replied in disgust. "I don't want our son growing up in an apartment. I already have a home for him to live in where he'll be safe and have a great childhood."

"You mean *our home*. I'm still part owner and you wouldn't have that home if it wasn't for me! This apartment is just a stepping stone. I plan to buy my own home in a couple of years, after the dust settles from our divorce. Deb, I really think you're being unreasonable here."

"It's you who are being unreasonable and selfish, like you always are. You only think about yourself and that's why I left your sorry ass.

Don't make me fight you on this. You already know the courts favor the mother when it comes to this sort of thing," Debra threatened.

Brian started to break out in sweat from anger, hurt, and betrayal. *This bitch is really trying to take my son from me,* he thought to himself. But he just didn't have it in him to vocalize his frustration. He had heard horror stories of the money wasted by good fathers in lawyers' fees only for the courts to side with the mother.

"Debra, don't, don't, don't do this!" he stammered, trying to hold back the hurt in his voice. Holding back tears, he managed, "We always agreed we'd do what is best for our son. He needs me and I need him. Please, don't try to take him away from me."

As soon as he finished his last sentence, tears came rushing out of his eyes.

"Are you crying, bro?" she said mockingly. "You are such a female..." She laughed. Then, she abruptly hung up.

Trying to regain his composure, Brian took a few silent breaths.

"Hello, hello...? Motherfucka!"

Brian dropped to his knees in the middle of the floor of his room and prayed while sobbing uncontrollably.

"Heavenly father, Lord Jesus, I come asking that you help me right now. I can't lose my son. I don't want him to experience what I did growing up, not really knowing his father. Lord, please soften Debra's heart. I'm not sure if I can survive this. Help me, Lord, please... please...please," he whispered.

With his face pressed to the carpet and tears soaking it, and snot coming from his nose, Brian whispered to his God and tried to comfort himself from the pending calamity that awaited him and his son. He cried so hard he developed a headache. He stayed in a fetal position on the floor for over an hour, dozing in and out of sleep, hoping this was just a bad dream. Then, suddenly, his cell phone made another loud *buzz* sound. It was a notification that a new video had been uploaded to YouTube. The buzz startled him a bit, enough to make him get up from the hotel carpet. He grabbed his phone. He squinted to read his screen. His eyesight was still blurry from his tears but he managed to get a glimpse that the video was a new Breakfast Club interview featuring Philip "Sharp Skills" Jacobs. Brian was about to put his phone down to go back and lay on the floor, but he caught a glimpse of the headline: Philip "Sharp Skills" Jacobs talks divorce, fatherhood, mental toughness, and new venture, Gladiator School."

Brian had heard a few of this guy's songs and thought they were pretty good, but didn't really follow him otherwise. But that headline caught his attention. He grabbed his Beats headphones so he could listen. Maybe this would help answer some of his questions about the current drama in his life.

                    DJ ENVY
          Good morniiiing, we are your hosts
          DJ Envy, Charlamagne the God, and
          Angela Yee. We are the Breakfast
          Club. We have a very special guest in
          the building, Philip "Sharp Skills"
          Jacobs.

                  CHARLAMAGNE THE GÓD
          Good brother, Sharp.

                                        CUT TO:

          SHARP SKILLS is wearing a puffy red-and-black
          Rebel Firm coat that flawlessly matches a black
          cashmere sweater. He wears a glimmering-gold
          Rolex presidential watch on his right wrist. He
          is adorned like a modern-day king. His tone is
          confident, yet he has a humble aura about him.

### SHARP SKILLS

Good morning, good morning. Wow, this is a real dream come true. A long time getting up here with ya'll. I'm honored.

### CHARLAMAGNE THE GOD

Glad you are here brother. I recently found out about you and all the incredible work you have been putting in for years. I'm not sure how talent like yours goes unnoticed for so long. Your body of work is impressive. Let's just go down the list real quick for the listeners, because many of them probably don't know who you are. You've written nine books, nine! Released over twelve albums. I listened to the last three releases, incredible music by the way. You have a board game you created, and you run a global consulting firm called Rebel Firm. And, you have managed to do this all independently. Wow!

### SHARP SKILLS

That's a helluva intro, Charlamagne. You know man, I'm extremely blessed. I have a mother who instilled a deep sense of personal belief in me. I was raised to believe I could achieve anything I put my mind to. And, I'd say, God has ordered my steps in a way that forced me to bet on myself. It has been through some of my most difficult life circumstances that I leveled-up to the man I am today.

                    ANGELA YEE
I was reading your newest book,
*Gladiator*, and you talk about how your
divorce made you a better man. You
said that in your marriage, you were
not able to live up to your potential
but you didn't know it at the time.
Like, you were working hard, but
it felt like you were spinning your
wheels.

                    SHARP SKILLS
All facts, Angela. A bad relationship
can really stunt your growth. And
I'm not saying that as shade against
my ex-wife. We just weren't supposed
to be together, and when you are in
a relationship that is not meant for
you, it will limit your progress. Once
we were officially separated, I started
on the journey of self-rediscovery
and I feel like a completely new man.
Let me caveat this by saying, divorce
fucking sucks. I don't wish it on my
worst enemy because it will absolutely
leave a wound on your soul. Even
though my divorce was finished several
years ago, I still go to therapy once
a month. The longer the relationship,
the longer your healing process will
be, especially if it ends with a nasty
divorce.

                    DJ ENVY
Which yours was, right?

                    SHARP SKILLS
It absolutely was. You hope that if
you and your former partner can't

work things out in the relationship as it currently exists, maybe you can make a peaceful exit. That didn't happen for me. And I think what makes it even messier is that when you've been married for so long - we were together for twelve years - you are tied together in ways you don't realize until after you are separated. And that connection doesn't go away easily. You've been conditioned to be a certain way in a long term relationship and you have to relearn yourself, perhaps even learn yourself as an adult for the first time, depending on how young you were when you got married. So, there are a lot of different emotions that come with that, that I experienced internally and was the recipient of. If I'm being honest, I was also the deliverer of these emotions, myself. Divorce can bring out the worst in you. But I think I handled it the best way I could.

CHARLAMAGNE THE GOD
In *Gladiator* you talk about how the pressure you were under, which stemmed from your divorce, made you mentally stronger. Can you say more about that? I believe it's important for young people, young men especially, to hear that message. I feel like there are so many mentally and emotionally weak people out here today, and this is a big reason why there are so many tragedies taking place.

Absolutely. I feel like for the greater part of my life, I've always had a certain tenacity about me, but nothing taught me more mental and emotional toughness than my divorce. On a daily, no, hourly basis, I had to make the decision to not let my emotions take over my logic. I didn't always get it right, but I committed to the process. Let me break it down. I had to be mentally strong for my two sons, who were eight and five years old at the time. They still needed a solid father, regardless of what I was going through. They were also dealing with their own pain and hurt during the divorce. That pain still lingers up to the present day for them. I couldn't let my own woundedness scar them further by not showing up for them. Again, I didn't always get it right, and still don't sometimes. But I committed to the process of being a dad to my boys through thick and thin.

Then there's the battle that you go through in the courts. Attorneys are going to bleed you dry. Attorney fees probably aren't much money to y'all, but my divorce cost me $40K. I didn't just have that laying around at the time. So I watched my life savings dwindle to nothing while going through an emotional battle. I had to commit to the process of encouraging myself through this storm, constantly telling myself I would be able to get all that money back one way or

another, and then some. I would just
have to stay positive with myself and
keep believing in me. And the last
thing I'll say about this mental and
emotional toughness I developed was
that I went through a process where I
refused to give in to hardly any of my
vices.

I intentionally didn't drink any
alcohol for several months following
my marital separation because I knew I
needed my judgment to be as clear as
possible. My judgment was foggy enough
already, from an emotional standpoint.
Also, alcoholism runs on certain sides
of my family and I saw the effects it
had on some of my people. Motivated by
my sons' stability, I decided I didn't
want them to experience that kind of
turmoil. I felt like alcoholism was a
cycle that needed to be broken.

Brian shifted on his bed from discomfort. What Sharp said hit home
for him, especially because he was gripping a bottle of whiskey as he
listened to the interview.

SHARP SKILLS
I also intentionally did not date any
women for several months immediately
following my separation. I wanted
to, but I knew I needed to heal or
I would attract a similar or even
worse relationship into my life. We
attract what we are, not what we want.

And my heart couldn't endure another
experience like the one I had during
my marriage and divorce. That really
sobered me up and got me focused in
that area of my life.

                    ANGELA YEE
        Are you dating now? Curious minds want
        to know.

                    SHARP SKILLS
        Let's just say I do alright in that
        arena. I'm not involved in anything
        serious because I'm so focused on
        my company. And honestly, I'm just
        enjoying the single life right now.

                    ANGELA YEE
        But you are dating?

                    CHARLAMAGNE THE GOD
        God damn, Angela, let the man
        breathe!"

The entire group laughs.

                    SHARP SKILLS
        I don't kiss and tell.

Everyone laughs again.

                    ANGELA YEE
                    (HINT OF FLIRTATION)
        That's okay, I'm gonna get you on the
        Red Lipstick Podcast and get you to
        open up, my brother.

Sharp Skills gives Angela full eye contact.

                    SHARP SKILLS
        I'm wit it, Angela.

DJ ENVY

It's heating up in here, let's
transition shall we? Let's talk about
your latest venture, the Gladiator
School, which is based on your book.
We didn't mention that this book has
sold *millions* of copies independently.
Definitely want to make sure we
highlight that. Out of all the things
you have created that you can promote,
you specifically wanted to talk about
this today.

SHARP SKILLS

Appreciate that, Envy. Yeah, based
on the astounding success of the
book, I felt like I really hit a
vein in society that had not been
tapped yet. And I thought building
some sort of a community of like-
minded people, Gladiators, if you
will, would be a great way to further
solidify the lessons I share in the
book. So I've set up these pop-up
Gladiator Schools that I host across
the country. And now we are getting
interest internationally, too. The
premise is that the Gladiator School
is a cohort of no more than eleven
people who I do an intense two-day
coaching session with to prepare them
for their journey of mental toughness.
These sessions are the launching pad
that will lead to mental, physical,
and spiritual transformation that the
Gladiators can use for the rest of
their life, so long as they maintain
the regimen my team and I provide them
with. The results are really up to

the Gladiators. Their success depends on how deeply they lean into the training and stick with it after we conclude. The dope thing is that they have access to the content after the sessions and we have a community of trainers they book coaching sessions with if they so choose.

DJ ENVY

What are some of the things that you cover in the sessions?

SHARP SKILLS

I walk the gladiators-in-training through everything I did to become the man I am today. I share my:

* Workout and eating regimen.
* Finance and investing regimen.
* Professional and career progression regimen.
* Goal setting and vision board creation regimen.
* Books I have read and other forms of content I consume on a regular basis.
* My productivity schedule, which will enable them to bring their dreams to reality.
* My spiritual practices.
* Angela Yee will like this one: my approach to dating and relationships.
* This is a big one: my affirmation regimen.

                    CHARLAMAGNE THE GOD
          That sounds dope and equally
          expensive.

Everyone laughs.

                    SHARP SKILLS
          Well, it's not cheap. But the way I
          see it, what is your mental toughness
          and overall mental health worth?

                    CHARLAMAGNE THE GOD
          Priceless.

                    SHARP SKILLS
          Exactly. To me, it's more expensive
          to live a shell of an existence than
          it is to make an investment of money,
          time, and energy that will transform
          you forever. You are your number one
          asset.

                    DJ ENVY
          Well said. Well, on that note, we
          know you have to get out of here
          because you have a crazy press run to
          continue while you're in New York. We
          appreciate you for being here with us
          today, dropping gems, being authentic,
          and doing the good work that you do.
          Before you go, please tell the people
          how they can find out more information
          about Gladiator School and Rebel Firm,
          in general.

                    SHARP SKILLS
          They can go to rebelfirm.com for
          everything. And I am honored to have
          been able to hang out with you guys.
          This was dope.

CHARLAMAGNE THE GOD
It certainly won't be the last time,
you a solid brother.

Well, ladies and gentlemen, there you
have it. Philip "Sharp Skills" Jacobs.
And we are the Breakfast Club, good
morning!

Brian put his bottle of alcohol down and took a deep breath. That short interview inspired him more than anything else in the last several years. He felt like he was starting to form a gameplan. And he was going to figure out a way to get into the Gladiator School. He knew he needed to be a part of that community. With his newfound motivation, he threw on a sweatsuit and his sneakers and went to the gym.

# SICKNESS

**T**anya massaged her temples as she sat in the bath tub soaking after another exhausting day of work. She hated her job, but it paid the bills, she reasoned to herself. She looked at the time on her phone. It was 9:48 pm. In another six hours she would have to get up without enough sleep, yet again, with an almost two-hour commute to the office. It wasn't so much the work she did that she despised, it was the work environment. She had petty and passive aggressive co-workers.

Tanya did her best to keep her head down and work hard, but she always ended up in some sort of drama with her co-workers. Couple that with sleep deprivation and she started to feel miserable every day. She laid back further in the tub, almost falling asleep until her older sister, Tracy, came barging into the bathroom. She and Tracy were roommates.

"What is it?" Tanya asked with a scowl on her face.

"I need to borrow $100," Tracy said, her voice full of entitlement.

"You still haven't paid me back the $250 I loaned to you a month ago, and you have not helped out with rent in like, six months. No, I can't do it," Tanya said. She closed her eyes, trying to relax again.

"I know you got it, I need it for something very important," Tracy said.

Tanya was used to Tracy either bullying or manipulating her into doing what she wanted, a skill Tracy had cultivated over the last several years.

"I said I don't have it," Tanya shot back with all the resolve she could muster. She was somewhat afraid of her older sister and usually gave in to her demands because she had been conditioned to do so since they were kids.

Tanya began to shake, an occurrence that happened more and more over the last five months. Sometimes, these shakes were severe, and if she was driving, she'd have to pull over on the side of the road. She also experienced migraines. She worked the majority of her day because her job was demanding. It didn't pay enough, though, which led to her working more hours and stressing out over bills. With all these stressors and ailments, Tanya knew she needed medical help.

A few months prior, she began to get recurring thoughts about dying before the age of thirty. These thoughts came so often she began to believe they were originating from herself. She slowly began to accept them as fact. As a result, she wasn't taking as good of care of herself as she knew she should. She ate fast food almost everyday of the week, accepted mistreatment from others (especially her sister), and didn't work out. When she looked in the mirror, she was not proud of what she saw, although she was a beautiful woman by most standards.

Tracy scoffed. "I know you got it!" she yelled before storming out of the bathroom.

Tanya heard her storm down the hall and go into Tanya's room. Tanya knew Tracy would start going through her stuff to find money. Tanya could hear her from the bathroom, but she was too beat down, mentally and physically, to do anything about it. She just sank lower into the tub as if she was hiding.

"I found $100, you lying bitch! I'm taking this. I will pay you back. You really need to stop lying and get your life together," Tracy fired.

Tanya began to quietly weep. She was tired of her sister, tired of her job, tired of stressing about the bills, and tired of being sick. After about twenty minutes of silently sobbing and soaking in the tub, she finally got out, dried herself off, and put on her robe. She went to her room, which had, in fact, been ransacked by Tracy. She didn't even bother to clean it back up. Instead, she grabbed a blanket off the floor, wrapped herself up in it, and turned off the light before laying down. As she closed her eyes, the negative thoughts she'd been experiencing came back to her.

*You're not gonna make it, Tanya. As bad as you feel, there's absolutely no way you're going to see thirty. No kids, no marriage, no career in the cards for you. You're so frail, brittle, and sickly. You're going to die soon!*

The thoughts came rolling in. They wouldn't stop. Tanya became sick to her stomach and had to run into the bathroom to vomit up the leftovers of Chinese food she'd eaten for dinner. The stress she was under was causing nausea and literally killing her, she knew. Then, an unfamiliar thought came into her mind.

*Nobody's coming to rescue me. If I want to live and live my life to the fullest, I'm going to have to make it happen.*

Even as she crouched over the toilet, she felt a strange sense of empowerment. But, she had no clue where to start the work of getting her life together. She was not a deeply religious person, but she did believe in a higher power. She whispered with utter sincerity into the darkness of the bathroom.

"If there is someone up there, please help me figure this out."

As she got up to head back into her room, she heard her phone chime. She went over to it and looked at it. She'd received a YouTube notification about a new Trevor Noah Daily Show interview. His guest was Philip "Sharp Skills" Jacobs. The title read, *Overcoming dark seasons in your life*. She had never heard of Philip "Sharp Skills" Jacobs before, but the title intrigued her and she was a big fan of Trevor Noah. She tapped play on her phone.

```
                    TREVOR NOAH
          Everybody give it up for the legendary
          Philip 'Sharp Skills' Jacobs.

     The CROWD applauds enthusiastically.
```

Tanya watched as Sharp came out to the interview couch, smiling from ear to ear. He waved at the crowd and made praying hand gestures to them.

```
                    TREVOR NOAH
                      (warmly)
          Wow, what a reception! Now, I've got
          to tell you Sharp, a lot of people
          have come and sat on this couch, and
          dare I say many more well known than
          you, but I can tell by the audience's
          reaction that you are loved.

     More shouts come from the AUDIENCE.
```

                    SHARP SKILLS
          I'm humbled and honored, Trevor. I'm
          just taking it all in.

                    TREVOR NOAH
          You should, brotha, you are doing a
          lot of good in this world that has
          gone under the radar for a long time.

The AUDIENCE erupts into cheers and praise.

                    TREVOR NOAH
          Now, I've been following you and
          your journey for quite some time,
          probably unbeknownst to you. But
          you have inspired me from afar for
          a couple years now. Your drive, your
          motivation, and your consistency are
          highly admirable. But what I've been
          most impressed by is the integrity
          you've demonstrated in your life. We
          are going to discuss your new venture,
          Gladiator School, in just a moment,
          but I wanted to give you flowers while
          you can still smell them. Black man to
          Black man.

TREVOR and SHARP reach out to each other for a
heartfelt bro hug. The AUDIENCE cheers again.

                    SHARP SKILLS
          Thank you, Trev. That means the world
          to me. My road has not been easy,
          but I am extremely grateful for the
          journey and who it has turned me into.
          I'm also honored to know I've inspired
          you in some small way. That is one of

my goals: every day I want to inspire someone.

At this point, Tanya was hooked. There was something about the way Philip spoke that resonated with her. She sensed he had been through hell, but he didn't have any burns on him. He spoke with a quiet, yet strong inner confidence that can't be faked.

                    TREVOR NOAH
          Let's talk about Gladiator School
          and the whole ecosystem of personal
          development you are building through
          it. What inspired you to create this
          program?

                    SHARP SKILLS
                      (soft laugh)
          In short, bro, I've been through a
          lot of shit. But through it all,
          I managed to bounce back even
          stronger. So, I guess, combining
          my love for encouraging people and
          the many difficult life experiences
          I've encountered has birthed this
          ecosystem.

                    TREVOR NOAH
          Would you mind telling us about one
          of those difficult situations and how
          you were able to overcome it? I'm sure
          that would be highly beneficial to our
          audience.

                    SHARP SKILLS
          Most definitely. In Gladiator School,
          I talked about a time period when it

seemed like I just kept getting hit
with health challenge after health
challenge. My blood pressure was out
of control and I had a mysterious
itch that would ransack my entire
body several times a day. It wasn't
eczema, but I couldn't identify what
else it was. Years later, I came to
find out it was an allergic reaction
to my diet and a grooming product
line I had used for years, and heat
amplified the adverse reaction I was
having to it. I also went through
bouts of mental trauma because of a
very toxic work environment that I
was in for over five years. On top of
all this, I wasn't eating right and
was not really taking the best care
of myself. I remember those itching
spells were debilitating, and the
only thing that would sooth me was
rubbing something cold on my body.
I was always so embarrassed when it
happened. I used to go to the barber
with an ice cold bottle of water for
when an unpredictable urge to scratch
would surface. I would have to hold
back from scratching until it passed,
so I didn't look crazy. It was sheer
torture, man. I remember thinking to
myself, how can I possibly live like
this for the rest of my life? Any time
I sweated or felt hot, I'd need to
scratch myself like a crackhead.

The AUDIENCE laughs.

Tanya felt strangely seen. Although the types of health challenges she was facing were not exactly the same as Sharp's, he was still speaking her life story.

### SHARP SKILLS

It was in those time periods of my life that I had to find something to live for, and I had to believe I could overcome those challenges. It was really my self-belief and a persistent motivation to improve my health that got me through. I got to the point where I would intentionally put myself in hot rooms and environments to condition my body to face the heat and that crazy-ass itch. I purposely leaned into the discomfort so I could master it instead of letting it dictate how I would move through life. I'm not gonna lie, that shit was hard. But for the sake of my kids and also my own future, I knew I had to pull through or all of these issues would end up turning me into a shell of a man.

There's a story about Jesus healing a man who had been paralyzed for several years because the man couldn't get to a pool of water that healed people. One of the first questions Jesus asked him was, 'Do you want to be healed?' That question was critical, because often, we get beaten down by life for so long that we lose the will to fight for a better life. And we no longer have the mental fortitude to

```
participate in our own rescue. And
there's just something in me, bro,
that won't let me quit on myself.
Maybe I'm special in that way, but I'd
like to believe that every human has
that quality inside themself. It might
take someone or something to awaken it
inside us, though.

This is the primary reason I wrote
Gladiator and started the Gladiator
School program. I want to help people
participate in their own rescue, and
then teach them to thrive once they've
risen out of the dark pit they've been
in.
```

```
The AUDIENCE cheers.
```

Tanya was in tears. Sharp was speaking to her soul and she felt more encouragement in that moment than she had in several years. She wasn't sure what her next steps were going to be, but she knew she would be able to move forward with her life if someone like Sharp could do it.

She understood she was going to have to make some tough changes, and implement them quickly. For starters, she needed to start taking better care of herself and really examine the stress triggers in her life. She also needed to set boundaries with her sister and people at work, and just about everyone she dealt with on a regular basis, from now on. Her peace was to become her first priority and anything or anyone that threatened it would have to go.

She heard Tracy snoring loudly in the next room. She thought to herself, *I can't wait to get this broad out of my house.*

TREVOR NOAH

So, tell us what we can expect from
this Gladiator School you've built?

SHARP SKILLS

Well, you can expect an immersive
experience, one that examines various
parts of our lives and what it takes
to develop a strong mindset in each
one. You'd be surprised what goes
into this. It's not just about being
physically tough and lifting weights
or exercising, although that is part
of it. The bigger picture examines
how someone takes care of their peace
of mind and their mental health.
You know, this includes taking care
of your body in ways like getting
massages, going to counseling,
and getting rest. I'm most excited
about exposing people to elements
of mental toughness that they might
consider 'soft' but which are crucial
to helping them develop the mental
strength and stability they need to be
at their best.

My team and I have laid out a
blueprint that will help people
get their lives back on track. And
not only that. Our program leaves
people in *better* shape than what
they previously experienced. The
program takes deep commitment, though.
People have to be able to identify
something they desire so badly that
they won't let anything or anyone
get in the way of having it. And they

have to use that desire to overcome
things like procrastination and
self-doubt. I had to overcome these
things personally, and even to this
day, I sometimes struggle to overcome
my own inclination to put things
off until the last minute. I battle
internal voices that tell me I can't
do something or that I won't do it.
But I reprogram myself every day and
take steps to ensure I continue this
process with longevity. And if I keep
at it, I see the results.

The first thing I cover with our
gladiators is vision. Everything
starts with a vision. What do you
see for yourself? Where do you want
to go? Why do you want it? This
last question is the most important
question to answer. Once people have
that understanding, we then look
at where they are in their life and
the repetitive actions they must
ingrain in themselves to realize
their vision. It all comes down to
repetition, and finding ways to get
better, incrementally, along the way.
This is where massive gains come from
down the road. My gladiators have to
have the long game in view because
significant improvement in one's mental
strength does not come overnight. But
if you follow the process we laid out
in gladiator school, you will look up
six months to a year later and be very
proud of the progress you've made. So,
I help people get really clear about
their vision. One of my favorite tools

to do this is with a vision board.
I've been using them for years.

                    TREVOR NOAH
I love vision boards. They serve as
powerful north stars for what you want
to accomplish.

                    SHARP SKILLS
Exactly. Moving something you envision
in your mind from a mere thought to a
physical representation that you can
look at everyday helps to center both
your conscience and subconscious mind
on what you want out of life. A few of
the pictures I had on my 2021 vision
board were related to how I wanted
my body to look and feel. That gave
me something to work toward. These
pictures on my vision board served
as reinforcements whenever things
presented themselves that were not in
alignment with my vision.

By this point, Tanya was taking notes and replaying central parts of the interview so she got every drop of information she could. It was 1:52 a.m. and she knew she was going to pay for not going to bed earlier. But, she also felt the wisdom she was getting was more than worth that price tag. She had never thought about creating a vision board for her life. She was always too caught up in the hustle and bustle, the hamster wheel of "just trying to make it." But with this newfound knowledge and motivation from the video she was watching, she felt empowered in a way she never had before. She wanted to take better care of herself. She had hard choices to make over the next few weeks. Namely, whether she would actually eat better, work out, go to therapy, kick her sister out, and get into a better work environment.

She knew it wasn't going to be easy, but things could no longer continue how they had. Tanya pulled out her laptop and opened up a blank Google Doc file. She stared at the blank page for a moment thinking about all the bullshit she had endured. She breathed deeply and closed her eyes, giving herself permission to dream of a better life than the one she was currently living. She thought about what a better version of her life might feel like, what she would wear, the places she would go, the work she would do, and the type of people she would allow to be in her inner circle. From there she began to look up images that reflected what she envisioned. She copied the images and pasted them to the document until she fell asleep.

# FINANCIAL TROUBLE

Lincoln rubbed his face in his palms as he looked at CashApp on his phone, awaiting a much needed $500 deposit for artwork he was commissioned to create for a close friend. His stomach grumbled and he thought about the irony of being a literal starving artist, barely able to feed himself two square meals a day. Since he decided to take the leap of faith on his dream to become a full time visual artist, the road had been very rocky. But at the age of twenty-six, he felt like it was now or never to live-out his passion. He wanted to bet on himself before the full weight of the responsibility that came with adulthood set in.

Lincoln was still single with no kids. He rented a room from an uncle who smoked a little too much weed but did well in the stock market after it recovered post the Great Recession of 2008. Although Lincoln's uncle was cool, he wanted his $800 a month on time, and Lincoln had been late on the rent the last four months. In the past, his uncle jokingly said he would evict Lincoln if he didn't get his money on time, but now there was a little less humor in his uncle's tone.

Lincoln dabbed his paintbrush in the crimson red paint on his art desk and applied another stroke to the canvas. He was creating a painting of a red sunset over a beach with turquoise, white, and dark blue waves receding back into the sea. He had a gift and he knew it, but his bank account hardly reflected that.

A louder-than-usual *bang, bang, bang* on his bedroom door jolted Lincoln, pulling him out of his painting session.

"Yeah Unc, come in," Lincoln said.

The door swung open and there stood Lincoln's 250-pound-plus Uncle Manny who was built like a linebacker and carried himself like it even though he never played football a day in his life.

"Lincoln, you know what day it is right?" Manny's deep baritone voice reverberated through the 150-square-foot room.

"Yeah, I know Unc. Look, I'm waiting on some money to come through. It should be here any day now. You see this painting I'm working on? The customer is sending me the deposit for it any minute, it just hasn't hit my CashApp yet. But I got you. I always get my rent in, even if it's a lil late."

"Lincoln, we are family, but I would've never let you move in if I knew things were going to be like this. You've been late pretty much every month since you've been living here. And now it's getting to the point that I feel disrespected. I did you a favor by not making you jump through all the hoops I would have made a regular tenant go through, but now I'm regretting that decision. I'm running a business here, not a daycare or shelter."

"I feel that Unc. I'm gonna make it up to you, I promise. I got some things lined up that are going to keep this from happening in the future."

Lincoln was lying, but he stuck to the story, anyway.

"That's what you've said virtually every month, Lincoln. You've just used different words. Look, you are a smart kid but don't try to play me for a fool. You are a man now, so I'm not going to baby you. You need to get your shit together or you are going to have a hard shake out here in the world. I'm going to give you one more pass and if you are late on the rent again, you are out of here, nephew. I'm sorry, but like I said, I'm not going to baby you. You've got to be held accountable as a man."

Uncle Manny turned around and walked off. Lincoln felt his heart drop down to the pit of his stomach when his uncle said those words. He had never truly been on his own before, or had to fend for himself. He was used to having someone in his family look out for him.

He tried to think of another place he could go. He didn't like the living situation with his mom and her boyfriend, so he knew he couldn't go back there. Living with them was more drama than he wanted to deal with, and plus he did have pride. What business did a 26-year-old man have living with his mama?

He had a girlfriend who loved him dearly, but she was a bit clingy and he didn't want to be beholden to her for letting him stay there. Plus, he knew, to truly have her respect, or the respect of any woman, he needed to be able to stand on his own two feet as a man. It was tempting to just go play house with his girl, but he knew he would regret that decision in the long run.

"Where the fuck is that damn deposit?" He muttered to himself through a clenched jaw.

He checked his phone again to see if the CashApp notification had popped up, but nope, still nothing. He did get a notification that a podcast he followed, The Midnight Miracle, had a new episode out, though. The hosts Dave Chapelle and Mos Def were some of his favorite personalities. He loved listening to them and he saw they had a guest host today, Philip "Sharp Skills" Jacobs.

Recently, Lincoln had seen this guy pop-up on various internet platforms he visited, but he had never taken the time to listen. Today's podcast subject, "An Artist and Their Relationship with Money," intrigued him. Lincoln put in his ear buds and situated his painting area so he could listen while he continued to work on the painting.

                    SHOW HOST
                 (deep, rich voice)
        Welcome to the Midnight Miracle, the
        greatest podcast on earth.

                  DAVE CHAPELLE
        Many times, as artists, we spend years
        perfecting our craft, sometimes to the
        detriment of making sure our financial
        foundation is set alongside it. I've
        seen so many creatives make this
        mistake. And that's why this episode
        of the Midnight Miracle holds a near
        and dear place in my heart.

                    MOS DEF
        Yeah, I feel that, my brotha. I think
        many artists, especially rappers in
        the era I was coming up in, didn't
        realize how profitable hip-hop could
        be, so we focused on *looking rich*
        instead of what it took to really *be
        rich*.

### DAVE CHAPELLE

We've seen the Jay-Z's, the Master P's, the J Prince's and how they've all managed to build business empires that stood the test of time. And I'm excited that a lot of the newer artists are capitalizing off their talent in similar ways. But in this episode, we want to discuss how the everyday artist, maybe the guy who doesn't have the biggest following or fame, can set themself up for financial success in an industry as fickle as the music business, and in the arts and entertainment industry, in general.

So, we decided to do something a little different on the show tonight. A few years ago, I met a very impressive rapper by the name of Sharp Skills at a nightclub I was hanging out at with some buddies in New York. It was right after I'd performed at Madison Square Garden. This nightclub was a low-key spot. That's part of the reason I ended up there. I like to have balance in my life, and after performing at the Garden, I wanted to be able to unwind in a nightclub that isn't well known.

So, we ended up at this little venue, probably held no more than 200 people, but it had a great vibe. We were chilling, drinking, and just having a good time. Then, the DJ brings Sharp Skills up to the stage. By his look, I could tell this guy was special. Not just because of the way he was dressed, but because of his demeanor, too. He looked like a professional, not just any Joe-no-name rapper. And let me tell you, this guy rocked the house! By the end of his set, Sharp Skills had everyone in the venue fixated on him, reciting his words like we had been hearing his music on the radio for years. I mean, I lost sight of how small the venue was and I felt like I was at a Jay-Z concert. The man put on an incredible performance. There was a richness in his music that I knew could only come from real life experience. I couldn't help but request an audience.

Sharp and I had the chance to chop it up for about 45 minutes in the green room. I learned that he was not only a hip hop artist, but an author, speaker, and entrepreneur. And in a day and age when many people are many things, he seemed to be executing in all these arenas at the highest level, despite not being widely known. I was impressed that he didn't ask me for anything. When most artists meet me, they want me to check out their music or take a picture to post on social media, some have even outright asked me for money to fund their vision.

CHAPELLE chuckles in his usual raspy way.

> DAVE CHAPELLE
> (continues)
> But Sharp was just a genuine dude and
> I felt like I was talking to a peer,

even though I knew he knew I'm much
richer than him.

EVERYONE laughs.

                    DAVE CHAPELLE
                    (continues)
        I felt like he was a kindred spirit
        and I told him I wanted to stay
        connected. We exchanged contact
        information, and on occasion, we
        would shoot each other a text to say
        hey. I'm always watching people who
        leave a mark on me, and so I kept an
        eye on Sharp and his progress as an
        artist, and as a businessman, really.
        So, when this topic of artistry and
        financial literacy naturally came up
        in our conversations, I immediately
        thought of Sharp. He is someone really
        living this stuff out and I think
        he's still at a level where his story
        and habits can still be relatable to
        up-and-coming creatives out there
        in the world. Although, I'm sure his
        net worth has increased significantly
        since our first encounter. But I'm not
        pocket-watching out here...

The podcast CREW laughs.

                    DAVE CHAPELLE
                    (continues)
        So without further adieu, Sharp
        Skills, everyone!

                    SHARP SKILLS
        Thanks, Dave. I appreciate this
        opportunity, my guy. And my net worth

                    is exactly the same as when we met,
                    especially if my ex-wife is listening.

SHARP's smirk is audible.

                              MOS DEF
                    I hear you on that, my brotha. So tell
                    us about you and how you approach the
                    financial space as an artist.

                              SHARP SKILLS
                    If I have time, I'll take ya'll on the
                    scenic route of my journey.

                              MOS DEF
                    Please do.

                              SHARP SKILLS
                    There's been a few defining moments
                    for me which have shaped how I've
                    been influenced by and made passionate
                    about financial literacy. The first one
                    is when I was introduced to Robert
                    Kiyosaki's book, *Rich Dad Poor Dad*,
                    when I was around sixteen years old.
                    I have an older brother, who at the
                    time, was locked up. He would write
                    to me from prison and tell me the
                    importance of understanding money. He
                    advised me to start reading the *Wall
                    Street Journal* to become familiar with
                    the terminology and overall climate of
                    finance in this country. Growing up,
                    my brother was my idol, so I probably
                    would've done anything he asked me to,
                    and so I was lucky he gave me that
                    good advice. I took it and ran with
                    it at a young age. Plus, I always
                    remember my brother having money and
                    nice things, although now that I think

of it, some of it was probably gotten from less-than-ethical means. Anyway, he motivated me to start learning about money.

I'd say the second experience that shaped my relationship to money happened through college. I have a degree in business administration, and the reason I chose that as my major was because I wanted to build structure around my music and creativity. I felt like I had creativity in abundance, but I needed a system for it if I was ever going to make a living from it. That was my entire rationale for going to college. I was fortunate to be able to have intentionality and a real world project that I could focus on while I was in school. That made my college journey a lot more meaningful. While I was in college, I dropped one of my more popular albums, "The Campaign," and had a huge release concert. This gave me hands-on experience of being a creative entrepreneur. One of the songs, The Mountain Movement, got a major placement in the trailer of a movie, Takers, and I started getting my first royalty checks.

All of this stuff was happening around the same time and I began formulating how I wanted my financial situation to be very early on in my career. I wasn't balling, but I was seeing more money than I ever had before and some of the education I was getting while I was in school just kept planting more seeds on what was financially possible.

Before people start thinking I had it made, though, the year prior to that, I was in one of the worst financial positions I had ever been in. It was so bad that I couldn't afford books during one of my quarters at school. I'll never forget having to borrow an older edition of a book for a marketing class from my professor. That shit was so embarrassing. But, I had to do what I had to. And speaking of intentionality, again, I ended up doing really well in that class because it forced me to study harder since I knew I was at a disadvantage with an outdated book. This taught me how to do more with less. Which is one of the principles I want to pass on to your listeners. It's not always about having the most top-of-the-line stuff, but using what you have to its maximum potential, instead. This often yields greater results. And, once you see a significant return on investment by using what you already have to the best of your ability, it is a natural part of the process to grow and expand from there.

A lot of creatives either make the mistake of underinvesting or overinvesting in their craft. By underinvesting, I mean they are not putting forth the time, effort, and financial resources to position themselves for greater growth. By

overinvesting, I mean they can go
out and spend too much time, effort,
and financial resources on something
that they may not stick with in the
long term. There's a balance that
must be attained. Here is my advice,
simplified:

* Start with what you have
* Maximize what you have
* Grow your enterprise or venture from
  there
* Rinse and repeat

Lincoln was so caught up in the knowledge Sharp was sharing that he didn't realize he had been painting the same area of the canvas for the last ten minutes. He came to, switched the colors on his brush, and began working on the middle section of the canvas.

SHARP SKILLS
(continues)

The third part of my journey I want
to highlight was a paradigm-shifting
conversation I had with my cousin. At
the time, I was just about to graduate
college, I had just met my future (ex)
wife, and I was getting ready to move
back to L.A. I shared with my cousin
my aspirations of becoming a rich and
world-famous rapper. I told him I
was going to Cali, where I was going
to try my hand at doing music full
time. My cousin, who is about fifteen
years older than me, sat quietly in

the driver seat for a moment. Then lovingly but firmly, he told me I needed to get a job. My heart sank. And I was so mad at him for saying that.

DAVE CHAPELLE
This shit is getting good. What happened next?

SHARP SKILLS
My cousin explained that the music business is fickle and LA is a hard place to make it. He didn't say that because he didn't believe in me. He said it because he didn't want me to struggle. He said I needed a financial base in order to invest in my dream.

'Don't give up on my dream, but be practical, too,' he said. I would need a place to stay, food to eat, clothes to wear, a method of transportation, etc. And on top of all that, I was getting ready to get married.

Looking back on that advice, I can see it was just what I needed to hear. It wasn't what I wanted. But, it proved to be invaluable all these years later. Because I've always had a strong financial base, I was able to fund my vision without being homeless. Sometimes, I was frustrated because I wanted to work more on my craft than I wanted to put in hours for somebody else's vision, but that's where a tough mindset comes into play.

If you have a legitimate dream, you will still think about it even when you are doing other things. And those other things will serve your dream in some capacity. For example, my commute to work was disgusting in those days. The first job I took in California was as an energy auditor. I had to drive two hours to work and back each day because of where me and my (ex)wife lived. On top of that, I had to drive around town all day to do inspections. Instead of complaining about it, though, I listened to beats while driving and wrote my rhymes during my breaks. I also began checking out audiobooks from the library and listening to personal development content in between meetings with clients. Because of my determination and focus, I was able to release two music projects and my first book while working that job. So, technically, I didn't miss a beat, all pun intended.

Now, my journey is not everybody else's. Some people might argue that to pursue your dream, you need unfettered time and focus. I say, if you have that luxury, more power to you. I didn't, though, and I don't regret that. Working while pursuing my artistry enabled me to:

* Fund my vision
* Mature as a man and creative
* Manage a budget and schedule
* Maximize my time

- ⋆ Save and invest money
- ⋆ Take care of myself and my family consistently.

This was something Lincoln did not want to hear, but he knew he needed this advice the same way Sharp did when he was a young, up-and-coming creative. Lincoln appreciated that Sharp acknowledged his journey was not the same as everybody else's and his advice was not a one-size-fits-all solution. Still, there were gems in what he shared that could be applied to everyone, like the fact that to be successful in any endeavor, there needs to be structure around creativity, intentionality to maximize what you have, and a consistent way to fund your vision and take care of your basic needs in the process. Message delivered.

Lincoln sat down on his bed and paused the podcast episode. He planned to return to it, but he wanted to reflect on what he'd just heard and how it applied to his current situation. He pulled a notepad he used for sketches and other creative ideas out of his backpack. He opened it to a new page and wrote at the top, *Things I need to do to become financially stable.* He thought for a moment, then listed what he thought he needed:

- A regular and consistent amount of income, either through a job or some other service I can offer the world that people would reliably pay for.
- Savings of at least $5,000. This number is a stretch goal for me, but attainable by the end of the year.
- Paying off debt, starting with the smallest balances and then working on the larger balances. I have about $7,000 in credit card debt. I don't feel too bad about the debt because much

of it was used to fund my artistry, but I know I need to get it under control, especially since the income I make from art is inconsistent right now.

After he wrote these out, Lincoln took a deep breath. He knew he had some work to do and it involved some things he really didn't want to do. But he resolved in his mind that he was going to use the process of becoming financially stable to set himself up for the future success he desired. He then began to write what he wanted to be happy and successful in life:

- To not have to worry about money, so I can create art from a pure place.
- To charge $5,000 and above for commissioned paintings.
- To travel to different art galleries around the world.
- To have my own art gallery.
- To earn at least six-figures a year from my art.

Lincoln carefully studied what he wrote down for each list and said to himself, "Sometimes, you gotta do the things you don't want to do now so you can do everything you want in the future." He grabbed his hoodie, turned the podcast episode back on, and went outside to take a walk.

# IDENTITY CRISIS

Layla gazed off into space as she sat in her 2019 Lexus in her driveway. She wasn't quite ready to step into mom mode and tend to her three daughters after a long day at work. Her husband, Jeff, worked remotely from home, so their girls were cared for while she sat in her car. They flooded Layla with attention every day when she got home. Layla also tended to be the more fun parent, so the girls naturally gravitated toward her.

Over the past few weeks, Layla was experiencing a sense of dread about her life. From the outside looking in, she had it made. She and Jeff made great money, they lived in a middle-upper-class neighborhood, she had an enviable career as a vice president of a top-tier consulting firm, and she had a beautiful family.

*What's wrong with me?* she thought to herself.

She had a lot of friends in her network, but none she felt safe expressing her frustrations about life with. She was the most financially well-off and had the reputation of "having it all together." She felt trapped, almost as if she had been living a facade for the last fifteen years she had been married. She had a deep, nagging sense that she wasn't being true to herself and hadn't been in a long time. But she wasn't sure how to articulate this to her husband. She loved Jeff, but she was tired of the same old routine their life together had cultivated. Her weeks blurred together when she followed her routine:

- Work an average of 50+ hours a week
- Go to the Women's Sports Club or do extracurricular activities every Monday, Wednesday, Thursday, and Saturday
- Family movie night on Friday
- Church on Sunday
- Family dinner on Sunday afternoon

Same ol', same ol'. The monotony was starting to drive her crazy and she could tell because her fuse was becoming much shorter with her friends and family these days. Before marriage and having a family, Layla was much more adventurous, and even a little wild. But, she had put that part of herself on the shelf for the sake of being a "good wife and mother."

She didn't want to blow up her family, and she knew divorce wasn't the answer, but she felt something deep in the pit of her stomach saying she needed a change or she was going to crash somehow.

She texted Jeff. "Hey babe, I need some time before I come into the house, I'm going to make a couple stops and be home in about an hour."

"Is everything alright?" Jeff texted back.

*He is such a good guy.* she thought.

"Yeah, I just need a moment," she texted.

"Okay ♥."

Layla wasn't used to having extra time on her hands and she didn't really know where to go, so she just drove. She passed several lights and then saw The Gasser, a local bar in a sketchy part of town. She often saw bikers go in there. The place had never caught her eye until today. She drove into the parking lot. She was in an expensive business suit and was not dressed for the occasion. She took off her coat, unbuttoned a few of the top buttons on her blouse, and frazzled her hair. One of the bikers caught her primping and smirked at her. She was embarrassed, but she told herself, "I'm doing this."

She got out of her luxury SUV and walked through the parking lot in her $2500 Hermes pumps. She opened the door and accidentally bumped a large, heavy-set biker wearing a cut-off jean jacket that revealed two arms totally covered in tattoos.

"Oh, I'm so sorry," she blurted.

The biker looked her up and down and just grunted. She eased past him. There was a lot of activity inside the bar: people were shooting pool, throwing darts, laughing, cussing, and shit-talking. Layla was totally out of her element, but she loved it. She sat down on a stool at the bar and looked at the bartender, a slender, tatted-up brunette with hazel eyes and lip and nose piercings. She was very attractive but had a look of, "don't fuck with me." She was talking to one of the patrons, who appeared to be a regular. She paid Layla no mind.

Layla sat patiently at the bar for about five minutes, hoping to get the bartender's attention, but the bartender did not budge from her conversation with the patron. It seemed like she was ignoring Layla on purpose. Layla was not used to being ignored. She felt disrespected and she knew she needed to get home soon. After another minute or two, she couldn't stand being ignored any longer.

"Excuse me, what does a person have to do to get a drink here?"

The bartender turned around slowly, with a sly grin on her face. "Hey, pretty lil thang, I'll get to you in a second." Then she turned right back around to finish her conversation.

Layla was flabbergasted. *Is this how things go in the wild?*

She got up to leave and the bartender called out, "Don't get your panties in a bunch, sweet thang. What are you drinking?"

Layla sat back down, a little unnerved by the bartender's sudden change in demeanor and customer service. She looked at the assortment of liquor bottles against the dark wooden casing.

"I'll have vodka and cranberry juice."

"No cranberry juice available, sweet thang."

The bartender grabbed a glass cup, revealing an art gallery of tattoos on her hands and arms. She tilted a bottle of vodka into the glass, poured straight, and roughly slammed the glass in front of Layla.

"Are you starting a tab or will this be your only drink, hun?"

Layla was getting irritated by the little nicknames the bartender kept giving her. She was only going to be so many more "sweet thangs, pretty lil thangs, and huns" before she snapped.

"This will be the only one," she replied without even looking at the bartender. She wanted the bartender to feel her irritation.

"Hmmm. Just what I thought..." the bartender replied with a chuckle. "That'll be eight bucks. Just leave it when you're done." She turned around, walked off and began talking with the patron at the other end of the bar again.

Layla was at her breaking point with this chick. She couldn't understand why this woman was disrespecting her like this. She told herself to ignore it and began to take sips of her drink, which she hated. She did not like drinking alcohol without a chaser. But she wasn't going to waste her eight dollars. She drank it down in a couple hard and forced gulps.

Layla reminisced on the days of her youth, when she was prone to getting into fights. She had a bad temper back then and it was something she had tucked away since moving into the corporate world and getting married. But, she did fantasize about how good it would feel to whoop this bartender's ass.

And then it happened. Layla came out of her fantasy as she heard the bartender say, "…bitch…" with a chuckle while giving Layla the side eye.

Before Layla gave one thought to her actions, she hurled her glass at the bartender, hitting her in the back of the shoulder. It shattered when it hit the ground.

The bartender hollered in pain and yelled out, "What the fuck was that for?"

"You tell me, bitch! Since I came into this hole-in-the-wall dust bucket of a bar, you have been utterly disrespectful! And then you had the nerve to call me a bitch. Well, I'm here now, we can get to the shits if you really want it."

Layla stood back from the bar anticipating the fight that was going to take place. She was ready to take out all her frustration on the bartender and let the entire world witness, if need be.

The patron spoke up, "She didn't call *you* a bitch. She called herself one because she's been having a rough week and she noticed how rude she has been to her customers lately."

The bar had gone silent as everyone inside listened to the exchange between the women.

"She glanced back at you because she was telling me that you looked like a nice lady and she felt bad for not being able to give you the level of service you deserved!" continued the patron at the end of the bar. "And, she keeps talking to me because I'm a trained psychologist…"

Layla was so embarrassed. The bartender was a tough woman, but her eyes were welling up with tears. Layla heard a booming voice from behind her.

Excuse me, miss, I'm going to have to ask you to leave," the big biker she had bumped into at the door loomed over her.

Layla was shocked at how professional his tone was. Everyone in the bar stared at her. She could not believe this was happening. She walked into this bar intimidated and afraid, and now was being asked to leave as if she was a menace to society.

"I'm sorry," she said to the bartender as she got up to leave.

The bartender rolled her eyes at Layla and started wiping down the counter, ignoring her. Layla solemnly walked through the bar to exit, then got into her car. She looked at her phone and saw several missed calls and texts from her family. And then she cried. She looked in her rearview mirror, taking in her reflection. She felt something she hadn't in a long time... lost.

"Yeah, babe," she said, answering Jeff's third call. "Yeah, I'm on my way home. I went to a bar up the street to unwind a little. It ended up not giving me what I thought I needed. I'll be home soon."

But Layla wasn't ready to go home just yet. She texted Jeff again. "I'm going to stop by the store on my way home. Do you want anything?"

"No thanks," he texted back.

Layla pulled up to a Walgreens not far from where she lived. She really didn't want anything, but figured she'd peruse the aisles. When she walked in, she went down the aisle the magazines were in. A cover caught her attention. A well-dressed Black man was on the front of *Entrepreneur Magazine,* the title read:

# Philip "Sharp Skills" Jacobs, the Modern Day Renaissance Man behind the Multi-Million Dollar Mental Toughness Empire, Gladiator School

The man on the cover was in a dark blue, pinstripe suit with aviator sunglasses on, a gold tie, and a crisp white shirt with gold cufflinks. He held a shiny gold, Spartan-style helmet with a bright red crest. Both the title and image stood out to her. She picked up the magazine and started thumbing through it until she got to the section with the article about "Sharp Skills." It was an interview. She skimmed it until a section in the article jumped out at her.

*Overcoming identity crisis and how to not self-sabotage in the process.*

**Entrepreneur:** *A core aspect of your Gladiator Training program is to help people strengthen their identities. Can you elaborate on why this is important?*

**Philip "Sharp Skills" Jacobs:** In my experience, knowing oneself is one of the most difficult things to accomplish in life's journey, especially for those who experience a radical change in their circumstances or intense discontentment at some point. And it's easy to let what we habitually do become the basis for how we define ourselves. We tend to do this without questioning or thinking deeply about whether or not our habits fulfill us. When someone does this for too long, they wake up one day and wonder who they are. This can be quite common for people with families, in relationships, or any context where they must focus on the wants and needs of others before themselves on a consistent basis. Obviously, it's important to consider the wants and needs of others, but not at the expense of losing yourself in the process. The goal is to find a balance, one where you remain true to who you are and provide value, love, high work performance, etc. to those you are responsible to.

When people hit the brick wall of identity crisis, they often make the mistake of feeling like they need to start from scratch in their lives, environments, and relationships. That is a decision they most likely will regret when their head catches up to their heart. You don't want to throw away all of the good you've built up and worked for in your life just because you have a temporary moment of feeling lost. You'll always be starting from zero if you give in to this urge.

I work with people on strengthening their identities so they are able to maintain their lives, especially the aspects they want to keep, while exploring the fundamental changes they are experiencing, which all humans do.

**Entrepreneur:** *How does mental toughness play a role in strengthening one's identity?*

**Jacobs:** I define mental toughness as having the ability to consistently push past your discomfort to achieve an outcome. When we have a goal, we need to push past the urge to disassociate from our current lives so we can hold on to what we've built and continue to be in healthy relationships we've established.

This isn't easy to do, especially when we are in the thick of feeling lost in our current reality. So, sometimes we have to do some unconventional things, things we wouldn't normally need to do, such as writing out a list of why we are grateful for the good people and circumstances in our lives, but which maybe we have taken for granted. This could look like either writing down or saying out loud what we are grateful for.

For instance, maybe you write down that you are grateful you can breathe without a tube down your throat. This moment of gratitude brings you to a place of reconnecting with the positive aspects of your life and shrinks the feeling of needing to dissociate completely. It won't eradicate an urge to escape entirely, but it's a start. Then let's say you then build up to writing down ten moments of gratitude throughout your day, which puts your mind in a place where it's saying, *I'm okay, everything is not so bad.* You then begin to reassociate more aspects of your life, in your current identity, to positivity.

The repetition of this skill builds up your mental toughness, or your ability to hold onto what's working in your life. Our habits form our identities. We become what we repeatedly do, as Aristotle put it. So, if there's good in your life, there are aspects of your identity that you'll want to keep so you can sustain the good even as you uncover new (or buried) aspects of your identity.

This brings hope because you are building character by not abandoning your responsibilities or the people who depend on you. Instead, you give yourself space to get to know yourself better in the process of transformation.

*It feels like Philip is reading my mail,* Layla thought to herself.

She still had questions about how to alleviate this feeling of being trapped in her reality, even though she had so much to be grateful for. She kept reading.

**Entrepreneur:** *Is there a time when it is right to leave your current situation, perhaps if the new identity emerging within you demands it?*

**Jacobs:** It's so cliché to give the answer I'm about to give, but it is appropriate. The answer is, it depends. If you're in danger or being harmed, especially intentional harm on a consistent basis, then you should absolutely leave your current situation. You need to get out of there. It will be healthier to cultivate a better version of yourself, a.k.a. your new identity, by pushing for a radical change. In those situations, radical change is necessary, both to escape a bad situation and to ensure you never go back to it. Leaving a bad situation can also protect you from others whom your wounded-ness and mental conditioning may have attracted. You will need to go through a long process of disassociating from that type of environment and those kinds of relationships to heal and redefine yourself. This will strengthen your identity so you don't fall victim to the same situation again. Many people are unable to break this loop for one reason or another.

On the flipside, if you are in an environment or relationship that is not harming you, you should really take a hard look at why you want to get out and what the ramifications will be if you leave. This is where being an adult becomes critical, because as an adult, you have to make decisions that are not solely in your best interests, especially when kids or other people who depend on you are involved. I'm not talking about people who are mooches and leeches, but people you have a responsibility to.

If you can think beyond where you are currently at and the emotions you feel in the moment, and envision the future, you can eventually get to a place where your identity crisis will make you a better person. An identity crisis signals a paradigm shift is occurring within you, but that doesn't mean you should leave what you have worked hard to attain.

Some people feel like they didn't have good childhoods or that they had to grow up quicker than they wanted to. And as a result, they want to experience a second childhood. I totally understand that feeling. But you can explore that inner child yearning to come out while also continuing to be a mature adult.

I'd say it's important to communicate with friends, family, and associates and ask for their support as you discover new aspects of yourself. But you have to stay reliable as much as possible in the process. That is key. Think of it like keeping your full time job, which pays all or majority of the bills, while you launch a new and promising side hustle. Over time, that new side hustle may become your new source of income, but until it is, you need to keep showing up for the occupation that guarantees your usual salary.

At that point, Layla closed the magazine. She had already been in the store much longer than she'd planned. She went to the checkout counter to buy the magazine, hopped in her car, and drove home.

She rode in complete silence thinking about Philip's words about the importance of staying reliable and communicating to loved ones about the internal changes she was going through. She was a little fearful, but felt even more liberated about the prospect of not having to let what she was feeling lie dormant inside her while also being able to hold onto her family and her career in the process.

She pulled into the driveway, took a deep breath, and walked into her home. She saw that the light in her bedroom was on, meaning Jeff was probably still awake. She stepped into the room, a little teary-eyed, and said, "Babe, we need to talk."

# ISOLATION

**T**ravis had had a long day at work putting out fires and solving personnel issues. He let out a heavy breath before he got out of his Dodge Challenger Scat Pack to go into the second party of the night he had been invited to. He had only come out of obligation, though. He was accompanied by a beautiful Thai and Black woman named Ashley who was one of several women he was dating. Travis was considered a modern-day "man's man" with an athletic physique, a high-paying career as a project manager in the construction field, and a sense of style that was unmatched in his peer group. He was a popular guy. But he was beginning to notice he was falling behind on his priorities of maintaining his gym regimen, keeping his house clean and organized, and budgeting his finances. His success was catching up to him and he wasn't doing what got him there.

He didn't feel like going to the party, but he promised his buddy Jaylen he would show up. Truth be told, he wasn't really into Ashley, either, but she tended to be available whenever he called and it didn't hurt that she looked incredible. He knew these were shallow reasons to keep hanging out with her, but he wasn't ready to settle down yet. He hadn't found a woman he felt he had a strong connection with.

He told himself, "Relax and have fun tonight. Don't overthink this."

He opened the door for Ashley. She stepped out with her long, bronze legs with gold, open-toed pumps revealing her meticulous pedicure. She wrapped her arm around Travis' as they walked to the front door of Jaylen's house. Hip Hop music could be heard from the street. The door was unlocked, so Travis and Ashley stepped inside. People were talking, laughing, drinking liquor, dancing, and smoking weed. It was one of Jaylen's typical parties.

"Trav, what up my boy?" yelled a high and tipsy Jaylen. "You made it. I was starting to think you weren't gonna show. I know you always got hella shit to do."

"Yeah, bro, I'm a man of my word. Unless something major happens, I show up to my commitments."

"My guy! Come on in. And who is this pretty lady?"

Ashley blushed. "I'm Ashley."

Jaylen reached out to shake her hand. He winked at her.

*Same old Jaylen, always trying to see if he can snatch my girl.* Travis thought to himself.

Travis and Jaylen had a long and complicated friendship. On one hand, they were childhood friends, but their relationship had always been marked by competition, mostly on the part of Jaylen. But Travis still valued him as a friend, nonetheless.

"You guys make yourselves at home. Drinks are over there, food is over there. Live your best life tonight."

Jaylen walked away to socialize with some other people.

Ashley sat down on a stool near where the drinks were, whipped out her cell phone, and started taking selfies. Travis looked at her in disbelief. He shook it off and went over to grab a drink. He looked around the room and saw a few familiar faces, but no one he was really tight with other than Jaylen.

There were a lot of people at the party, more people than Travis cared to be around. But a part of him hated being alone. When he was alone, he had to deal with himself and his inner turmoil. From the outside, he looked like he had everything put together. But on the inside, he constantly had the feeling he wasn't enough and that he needed to produce day-in and day-out in order to be loved. He was conscious of this dilemma, but could not break this mental cycle. He used work and surrounding himself with people to numb his pain. But tonight, he felt a shift.

He looked at his beautiful yet vain date, Ashley. He looked at his friend who lacked loyalty, Jaylen. And he looked around at the familiar faces at the party who he had no true connection with. He felt a deep sense of loneliness. He remembered hearing a speaker say that loneliness can be magnified in a room full of people because when you should feel the least lonely, you feel the weight of it even more.

"Just get through this night," he muttered to himself. Travis didn't realize it at the time, but he was ready for a fundamental change in his life that would require more loneliness, but it would result in him overcoming it.

After about an hour and a half at the party, Travis had enough of the fake environment. He tried to drink to loosen up, but even that didn't help him shake his feeling of loneliness.

"Ashley, let's get ready to roll."

Ashley was already very tipsy and got up, stumbling over to where he was at. Travis gave Jaylen the peace sign to signal they were leaving.

"Y'all out? Alight bro, thanks for coming through."

Jaylen eyed Ashley's butt as they walked out the door. Travis caught him staring. Jaylen looked up and smiled at Ashley and she gave him a seductive smile back.

As he opened the door for Ashley to let her into the car, Travis felt like he needed to get some things off his chest. But, he wasn't sure how to break it to Ashley. He knew for sure he didn't have a future with her. He also didn't like the prospect of being alone. Although he had other women he was dating, he somehow felt the most connected to her. On the way back to his place, he was in deep thought and unusually quiet.

"What's wrong, baby, you're super quiet?"

"Ah nothing, just got some things on my mind."

"Well, would you let me in your head? I wanna know what's going on with my man."

Travis let out a slight chuckle. "So I'm your man now, huh?" he said sarcastically.

"If you're not, then what are we then? Friends with benefits?"

"Ashley, I dig you a lot. More than I've dug anybody in a minute. But if I'm being honest, there's just something missing between us that I can't quite put my finger on. Maybe it's me. I've been thinking, maybe I need to spend some time just getting to know myself better, you know?"

"Are you breaking up with me?"

Travis took a long time to respond. He hated the thought of being alone, but he felt as if he had no alternative.

"Breaking up, no. Taking some time to come to myself, yes. I feel like I need to fly solo for a while."

Ashely started to sob. "Take me home."

Travis sighed, got off the freeway a few miles before his exit, and went in the other direction on the freeway. They didn't speak the rest of the drive.

When they pulled up to her house, Travis opened his door to get out and open Ashley's.

"I got it," she said sharply. She was obviously still hurt about them taking a break.

Travis, raised his hands off the door to signal he was honoring her wishes.

Ashley got out and slammed the car door.

"With an attitude like that, good riddance," Travis said to himself as he drove off.

He drove in deep contemplation as the white streetlights reflected through his windshield. He wondered about his life and what would be the outcome of this sudden change of heart. He also felt nervous about being totally alone. He wasn't good at that. But he knew he needed to get to know himself on a deeper level because no other person was ever going to make him happy and put him at peace. He reflected on all the girls he had been with in an attempt to fill a void and all the fake friendships he allowed just so he could feel like he was a part of something.

He laughed. "Am I having a midlife crisis?"

Then he got a text message from Ashley. It was a link to a YouTube video with, "I hope you find yourself" and a heart emoji below it. Travis was confused, one minute ago Ashley was pissed off at him and the next, she was sending him what seemed to be a positive closure text. He thought she might have been trying to be passive aggressive, but he opened the YouTube video anyway. It was a TEDx Talk entitled, "Why Isolation is Necessary for Great People" by Philip "Sharp Skills" Jacobs. Philip was wearing a well-fitting black tee, black jeans, and black and gold Jordan 1 sneakers that matched his gold presidential Rolex watch and Cuban link chain. Travis appreciated Philip's presentation, especially as a fellow man who liked to dress to impress. Once the audience stopped clapping, Philip launched into his talk.

## SHARP SKILLS

It does not come natural to the human species to be in isolation, especially for extended periods of time. We are relational and we are hardwired to be in community. So don't misconstrue what I am going to tell you about isolation, today. We need one another, but I'm here to share with you why, if you are a leader and or someone who wants to reach your fullest potential, you must go through certain periods of isolation despite that need for connection. I'm talking about spending time solely or mostly by yourself.

There is a unique inner confidence and self-reliance that comes from being alone if you maximize your time doing so. We live in a world where people are always looking for external validation and they can't function properly without it. But let me ask you a question. Let's say you were some sort of an artist, a painter maybe. And you feel like you just painted the dopest art piece of your lifetime, but there was no one to see it. Would you be okay with that?

I'd place a bet that many of you would not like the fact that you cannot share your masterpiece with another person.

But why is that? Why not be able to enjoy the painting whether or not someone else sees it? This is not an easy mindset to get to today, but it is critical to cultivate it if you want to be great and feel fulfilled with your life. Isolation, for a period, gives you the ability to only compare yourself against yourself, which is the only barometer of success worth obsessing over. Making progress against your former self is the most rewarding achievement you can obtain. While it feels good to outdo others in certain instances, for example, in sports or business, the satisfaction is fleeting. And it can make you obsess over things outside of your control, which can lead to a sense of worthlessness.

Isolation forces you to look at your greatest challenges, yourself, and then work toward becoming more than what you were yesterday, every single day. It forces you to figure things out on your own and develop a sense of trust in your own instincts, as opposed to relying on the guidance of other people, many of whom are making their best guesses in life, as well.

It was during my darkest moments that isolation actually became the breeding

ground for my greatness. I had to
learn how to encourage myself and be
my own support system. The confidence
I gained in that season of life
attracted higher quality people and
opportunities to me. I didn't have to
go searching for them, the vibration
and intention that I put out into the
world manifested it.

Travis stroked his chin in deep thought as he listened intently.

SHARP SKILLS
Isolation also gave me the courage to
walk away from harmful relationships
and turn down opportunities that were
no longer serving me. Oftentimes,
people stay in certain circumstances
because there is a sense of comfort
in the familiar, even if it is toxic
or stagnant. Or, they feel like
they can't do better. They allow a
self-limiting belief to become their
reality. You gotta bust through that
shit, you feel me!

The passion with which Philip spoke made the crowd erupt in
applause. The energy emanating through the video was palpable to
Travis. Philip was speaking truth that Travis needed at that moment.
Travis could feel the empowerment surging through his being,
motivating him for his journey of self-discovery.

## SHARP SKILLS

One critical thing you must make sure
to do while going through a process of
isolation is work on yourself. Just
being isolated will not improve your
situation. You must lock-in and focus
on becoming the best version of you
that you can become. You need to be
working out, reading self improvement
books, doing things and taking on
projects that feed your soul, and
when you do engage with other people,
practice social skills that improve
your standing with them.

Let me also say this: isolation
doesn't mean abandoning your spouse,
kids, and significant people in your
life. It means you are intentionally
taking time to focus on yourself
without interruption from other
people. One of the things I got really
good at because of my season of
isolation is hanging out by myself.
Sometimes, I would have so much fun
alone that people would come up to me
to see what I was about because of the
positive energy I was giving off. That
is literally power!

I want all of you to experience and
to know your personal greatness, and
isolation is one of the pathways to
get there. It is not the only one, but
it is one that has made a tremendous
difference in my life. I don't fear
being alone and because of that,

the relationships I do have are much richer.

When I create something, I no longer do it from a place of seeking outside validation, but from a place of purity and a love of manifesting something that once lived in my head. Don't get me wrong, external validation is appreciated, but it's not the motivation. Relying on the approval of other people will drive you crazy because we humans are fickle! Some people will see your passion, dedication, and skill for something but withhold acknowledgement simply because it's you.

Whereas somebody else they feel is 'safe' to them can do something of far lesser quality and be championed for it. When I saw this dynamic play out in my own life, I knew I had a choice to make. Either spend my life trying to convince others what I'm doing is valuable, or see the value in myself regardless of what other people think. And choosing to value myself has made a remarkable difference. Not only am I more centered in who I am and the direction I'm moving in, I'm also able to *become* and *do*, with more freedom and fearlessness. That's some gladiator shit!

Now there's a few things I need to tell you about isolation that are critical for you to know. You will have to resist the urge to get into

a relationship when you feel lonely.
Getting into a relationship when you
feel alone is something I would not
advise, because when you do, you enter
it from a place of neediness rather
than a place of strength. This makes
it easier for you to be manipulated
and to overlook major red flags that
can do tremendous damage to you
down the road. In those moments of
loneliness, my advice is to either
press through those emotions until
they pass, because they will, or go
hang out with people you know really
love and care about you, such as
friends, family, or even the dog.

In my opinion, it is better to learn
how to deal with loneliness on
your own so you can build a strong
foundation internally. Learn to rely
on yourself so that relationships with
other people will be an added bonus
to you rather than being based on
neediness.

While you are alone, read books, do
creative projects, work out, consume
information, and explore hobbies that
bring you joy. I turned my life into
a laboratory in which I would observe
how I and other people reacted to
certain situations. I learned a lot
about myself and continue to.

In closing, don't fear isolation. It
can make you great if you let it. Some
people willingly choose isolation,
others have to engage with it because

          that is what they are dealt. I've
          experienced both, and it made me a
          better human as a result. The same can
          be true for you.

Travis listened as the audience erupted with applause when Philip
finished his TEDx Talk. By this time, Travis had arrived home and
was sitting in his driveway. He looked up Philip's website to find
details for the next Gladiator School. He had to be there.

# HARD LIFE CHANGES

**C**rystal was finally at a place in life where she felt stable. She had her own place, a decent income through her job as an administrative assistant, a nicer used car, and she was able to pay her bills on time. Fourteen months prior, her life had been in shambles. At the time, she had no stable source of income and did not have consistent housing. She had been living between the apartments of her mother, sister, and cousin. When they had enough of her, she remembered the fear and embarrassment she felt as she went from homeless shelter to shelter and scraped money together doing a variety of jobs, like house cleaning, temp work, babysitting for her step brother, and filling out field research marketing surveys, which were few and far between.

As she made her thirty-minute commute to work, one of her favorite songs came on, "If You Try," by an artist called Sharp Skills.

It made her tear up thinking about how far she had come in the last fourteen months. She concentrated on the lyrics as she drove.

*"The culmination, now it's time to step out. Spent many years faith fighting to deflect doubt, sowed many seeds here and there for my late sprout, a modern-day Joseph in prison, vision to break out."*

She related to these lyrics. She had spent many years trying to establish herself but got knocked down by one life circumstance after another. But now, life felt different. She could breathe. She could think clearly.

When she pulled into her favorite parking spot at her job, she winked at herself in the rearview mirror. She was proud of herself. She looked herself over to make sure she was presentable to the world, then walked into the office full of confidence. As soon as she walked through the front door, she noticed many of her coworkers had a somber look on their faces. One was even quietly sobbing in her cubicle.

*Did somebody die?* She thought to herself.

Puzzled, she sat down at her desk and immediately fired up her computer. She scanned her emails and saw, *Ensuing Company Layoffs,* in one of the subject lines. Her heart dropped into her stomach. Somehow, she knew this email included her. She saw there was an emergency all hands meeting that would take place an hour from now. She kept reading.

*Dear Harbor Grove Medical Staff,*

*Due to recent downturns in the economy, which have severely impacted our business, we are forced to make the extremely difficult decision to lay-off a third of our workforce over the next two weeks. The company is not in a position to offer severance pay, however, if you have PTO available, we will compensate you for that.*

*We will have an all-hands meeting at 9:30 a.m. today to answer any questions you may have. It greatly pains me that you all have to experience this. I'm here to offer my support as you transition into other opportunities.*

*Sincerely,*

*Bob*
*CEO/President of Harbor Grove Medical*

Crystal sat in disbelief for a moment. She began to have visions of how her life was about to unravel all over again. She thought about how her credit score of 690, which she had fought to raise from 520, was going to drop again because she wouldn't be able to pay her bills on time. She was going to have to go back to doing random odd jobs to barely make ends meet while being drained in the process. She wouldn't be able to keep saving money and invest it into the stock market, like she'd planned. She had been saving money from every paycheck over the last several months and had plans of buying stocks with those savings every time her account reached $1,000. She was $347 away from being able to make her first purchase.

She started breathing heavily, as if she was about to have a panic attack.

"I can't believe this shit," she muttered under her breath.

Before she had a complete meltdown, the chief-operating officer of the company came into the main area of the office, where everyone was, and made an announcement.

"Hi everybody. Please make your way to the conference room for our all-hands meeting."

Everyone got up and made their way down the hallway and into the conference room to hear from the leadership team. Inside, Bob, the CEO, started things off.

"As many of you have already read in the email I sent out this morning, our company is in a very difficult financial position given the economic environment. Virtually all our clients are struggling to stay afloat, which has slowed our revenue. We are being forced to become a leaner organization if we hope to survive. We've done everything we can over the last eight months to keep everyone on board. But to be extremely candid, we've hit our breaking point. And the only way we can free up cash flow is to carry out the ensuing layoffs. We are going to do everything in our power to hire all or most of you back. But we must right the ship, first."

As the CEO spoke, Crystal tuned-out. The room turned blurry and the voice of the CEO began to sound like gibberish. She felt lightheaded and...

"Ma'am? Ma'am? Can you hear me?"

When Crystal regained consciousness, she realized she was laying on the floor with paramedics and her coworkers surrounding her.

"Oh my God, what happened?" she mustered from the floor.

"It looks like you fainted, ma'am," one paramedic responded.

"Bob was explaining the upcoming layoffs and you collapsed all of the sudden," said a nearby co-worker.

"Oh my God, how embarrassing. I'm so sorry. I'll be fine." Crystal tried to stand on her own.

She was still a little woozy, so the paramedics helped her get up. She took her time walking back to her desk. She could feel the paramedics keeping a close eye on her. She tried her best to look like everything was okay so she wouldn't have to be taken to the hospital. After about fifteen minutes, one of the paramedics came up to her.

"Based on our observation, we think you are in good shape. You may want to take the rest of the day off and just try to relax, though. We heard there are some pretty intense changes going on here. And taking some time to process might help you cope with them."

"I understand. Thank you," She said aloud.

Inside, she didn't feel like the paramedic's advice suited her. *It will be even harder to cope once I'm homeless and unemployed, she thought.* Eventually, the paramedics left and everyone migrated back to their cubicles and offices. Many people started packing boxes and taking their things to their cars. Crystal sat for a while in a daze until a coworker snapped her out of it.

"Are you going to just sit there feeling sorry for yourself?"said the woman.

"Excuse me, what?" Crystal said, trying not to reveal that her blood was beginning to boil.

How could this woman muster up the nerve to say something like this to her, given all she had been through within the last two hours? Crystal saw this woman from time to time in the office, but she never really said much and they had very limited interaction, if any at all. She was stunned by the woman's candid question.

"I know you don't know me from a can of paint," continued the woman, "but it was laid on my heart to share this with you." The woman handed Crystal a copy of Philip "Sharp Skills" Jacobs' book, *Gladiator*.

"I think you should start at Chapter 6. It is relevant to what you might be experiencing right now." Then the woman casually strolled off.

Crystal sat for a moment, studying the cover of the book, which had a helmet on it that looked like it was from the movie 300.

"Modern day parables for mental toughness" she read the subtitle aloud to herself as she inspected the front and back cover.

Then, suddenly, she put two and two together. Philip "Sharp Skills" Jacobs and Sharp Skills, whose music she happened to love, were the same person. She didn't know he was an author, too! Excitedly, she grabbed her purse and went to the stairwell in the building, a place she often went to get some alone time. She sat down and started to read Chapter 6, as the woman suggested.

# Chapter 6: Hard Life Changes

In 2013, I hit a real low in life. The company I was working for announced they had to start furloughing people due to their largest contract not getting renewed. I had experienced financial hardship before, but at the time, I had a wife and a new son who was only a few months old. I had to figure out how to make ends meet, and fast. What made this situation harder was its abruptness. I hadn't seen this professional change coming, so I didn't have an immediate plan for how to deal with it, nor significant savings.

I was scared, but ultimately, the situation caused me to stretch beyond my comfort zone. I applied for and received unemployment benefits and then made money from some side gigs. With that money combined, I was able to keep my family afloat. We may not have been able to go out to eat as much as we had before, but I was never late on rent. For a while, I went without buying new clothes and just did my best to maintain the clothes I already had.

I also had to learn how to be more resourceful and use my network more effectively. I started meeting new people to cultivate relationships that could be mutually beneficial to me professionally. I became bolder in advocating for what I needed, learning how to better negotiate (almost anything can be negotiated), and also starting to believe in my gifts and talents. A few years ago, right after I bought my house, I received word that the company whom my biggest contract was under was going to have to pause work for all of the subcontractors, including me. At the time, this contract provided the bulk of my income. Not only did I lose that work, but the future work in the pipeline they had slotted me for never materialized.

So there I was, with a new crib, much larger bills, and no solid income to speak of. I was scared as hell. But then I began to look at everything at my disposal, which were my talents of music, speaking, and facilitation. I also looked at the products I had created, several books, albums, and a board game. I realized I was sitting on a goldmine, I just had to be more intentional about putting myself out there. I had to adjust my strategy to make ends meet. I began to go out to networking events, which proved to be highly effective in opening new opportunities. I know everybody isn't sitting on multiple books, albums, and a board game like me, but everybody does have something to work with that they can monetize.

This unforeseen hardship showed me the importance of having a plan in case shit goes left. Your plan will not pan out exactly how you think it will, but it will give you a sense of direction when you feel lost and in the dark. Sometimes, unexpected crises come up that you can't plan for, but what you can do is make a plan in the midst of the hardship to give you clarity of thought and solidity of purpose. This solidity of purpose is also known as grit, the ability to stick with something even when it's tough. *Especially* when it's tough. Once you see the fruit of your labor, no matter how small, in the midst of a difficult life challenge, it will give you even more resolve and optimism to keep going in the direction you feel compelled to go in.

What I've discovered is that when I make up my mind to be diligent through a hard life change, I come out better on the other side in one way or another. Instead of fighting against it, I practice radical acceptance of the situation as it is, not what I want it to be. And because of this mindset shift, I can shift things to the outcome I want for the long run. There is power in being brutally honest about the situation you are in while maintaining the belief that it can and will change. We play a major role in what that change will look like by planting the seeds of the future fruit we hope to see in our lives. The real test is if you can keep planting and watering those seeds when the conditions of life seemingly fight against their growth. This is why most people give up and stay stuck.

I remember seeing a quote on an Instagram post that really resonated with me. I don't know who it's by, but it says,

"The best thing about life is that everything I've ever lost has been replaced with something better. I never lack, I just transition."

When I look back over my life, I find this to be true. In the worst of times, when I've held this mindset, I always produce a better outcome than at times when I focused on what I was "losing." So, I just want to encourage you to keep putting one foot in front of the other. What you are going through is not the end of the world, no matter how bad it seems. Try to stay as positive as possible and see this dark time as a dope-ass chapter in your book. You may even end up helping many other people going through a similar situation.

Reading this section of the book gave Crystal some hope that she could not only survive this hard life change, but thrive in the face of it. Her mind was opening to new ideas and strategies that gave her options about how to rise above past and present circumstances that had her feeling stuck. She felt as though she could dream again, and she began to feverishly write out how she wanted her life to look in the next six, twelve, and eighteen months. She closed the book, put her hands on her chin, and began to contemplate what her next moves might be. She knew one thing for sure: she would keep reading *Gladiator* and find out more about how to connect with Sharp Skills.

# NEWFOUND SUCCESS

**D**emitri felt like he needed somebody to pinch him as he looked out at the crowd of nearly 2,000 people packed into the concert venue, all of whom had come to see him perform. It had only been six months since he'd had a show but couldn't even get fifty people to come out to see it. But since then, a music video he'd created over two years ago suddenly went viral after Lebron James shared it in an Instagram story. Demitri had spent over ten years on his music grind and now, almost overnight, he was getting booked to play some of the largest festivals in the country.

His catalog of music had become the hottest, not only in his region, but across the United States, Canada, and Australia. His direct messages were full of attractive women vying for his attention, producers and other artists wanting to work with him, and music label representatives wanting to schedule meetings to potentially sign a contract with them.

All of his newfound success flashed in front of his eyes as the venue spotlights reflected off his Tom Ford sunglasses. He took a deep breath, then strummed the first note on his guitar. The crowd lost it. Before he sang one word, the audience started chanting his name. It was surreal to him.

"So this is what that feels like," he said to himself, recounting the many concerts he had been to where he saw some of his favorite performers cause fans to go into pandemonium simply by walking out on stage. That night, and as usual, Demitri got lost in his music and put on an incredible performance that left the crowd mesmerized. When he left the stage, his legion of fans chanted, "encore, encore, encore!"

He went back out on stage and saw a sea of phones out with their camera lights shining from them. He sat back down on the stool and performed another song, to the crowd's delight.

*I've really made it. I turned my dream into reality,* he thought to himself.

After his standing ovation and more encore chants, he gracefully walked off the stage. When he got backstage, Demitri was met by an aggressive man who was an artist manager for some famous artists he respected.

"Incredible show, man. Just phenomenal. You are definitely going places," the manager said with a devious smile.

"Thanks, I appreciate it," Demitri said hesitantly.

He was leery of the energy the manager gave off but was still high from his performance and doing his best to live in the moment.

"When you're ready to go to the next level, give me a call," the manager said. He handed Demitri his business card while a gorgeous woman came up to the manager and wrapped her arm through his.

She blew a seductive kiss at Demitri. The manager smirked as he and the woman turned away and walked off.

*That was weird*, Demitri thought to himself as he walked toward his green room. But he examined the manager's card, anyway and wondered what he'd meant by "going to the next level." Seeds of doubt began to spring up in his mind about the level of success he had just attained. He began to think maybe it wasn't enough. The manager's proposition piqued his interest.

Demitri walked into his green room, closed the door, and changed clothes.

"Great show tonight," the security guard said to Demitri as he walked out of the building to his car.

"Thanks bro, I appreciate you," Demitri said while signaling the peace sign to the stout security guard, who happened to be a Pacific Islander.

When he got in his car, Demitri looked at his phone and saw his social media was blowing up. He had hundreds of likes and messages about his concert. He still hadn't gotten used to his newfound success. He checked out a few comments on his post and then put the phone away so he could decompress while driving. He played his new album on his car stereo. It was an album he was currently working on. He usually listened to it everyday to see where he could improve it. But now he listened to it with a different ear because the concert he put on tonight really validated his confidence in his music. He gave himself permission to just zone out and enjoy his art.

Demitri arrived home before he knew it. He walked through his well laid out, yet modest apartment, dropped his keys on the counter, and plopped on his peanut butter brown couch. He looked around his apartment and a wave of discontent welled up inside him. He had just got done performing the largest concert of his life, yet he was all alone in a "small" apartment. He felt like he deserved more. More money, greater recognition of his talent, beautiful women (or at least one) on his arm, and a fun life. He thought about that manager he'd met, who had a beautiful woman with him and seemed to be living the high life. He wanted a piece of that.

"I want to go to the next level!" he said to himself out loud.

He went through his jacket pocket and found the manager's card. He texted him immediately. It was two a.m.

"Hey Rich, it's Demitri. Sorry for the late text, but I wanted to let you know that I'm interested in meeting with you to discuss what it might look like to work together."

About fifteen minutes later, Rich responded "If you're still up, me and some friends are grabbing drinks at the Lust Lounge. We'll be here for about another hour."

"Say less. That's not far from where I live. I'll be there in about 20 mins."

"Cool. See ya in a bit."

Demitri freshened up, splashed on some cologne, checked himself in the mirror, then headed for the door. When he hopped into his car, he received a notification that one of his favorite thought leaders, Philip "Sharp Skills" Jacobs, had just released a new video called, "Don't Let Em Trick You Out Ya Spot." Over the past several months, Sharp Skills had been releasing a video once a week, all of which were meant to inspire his listeners, of whom Demitri was an avid fan. Demitri opened the video on his phone and started watching it.

What's up Rebels, hope you all are doing well. I want to talk to you today about not letting people trick you out of your spot. Sometimes, we don't realize how good things are going for us and how "in position" we are. We live in a world that constantly communicates to us that we are not enough and we don't have significance. And there are so many swirling ideas about what success looks like that it is easy to get on the hamster wheel of always trying to prove ourselves. Even now, from time to time, I compare myself to others and think of all the places I don't "supposedly" measure up to my peers. I have to continuously refocus my attention on myself and the race I am running, taking my eyes off theirs, or I'll derail myself. I have to remind myself of what makes me great, unique, and impactful. I also must recommit myself to my process and programs I follow so I don't follow someone else's, especially those that don't suit me, no matter how attractive their results look to me. Oftentimes, their success is not what it appears to be, anyway. And if it is genuine success, their unique set of circumstances, background, acquired knowledge, skill, and opportunities place them where they are. I could not replicate their success even if I tried, nor could they replicate mine.

It is tragic when we don't celebrate our wins in life, especially the hardfought ones, because we are too distracted by the unsolicited opinions of others. It is a superpower to recognize and be proud of yourself, whether other people affirm you or not. What I've seen in my own life is that during some of my greatest moments, there is someone lurking in the background who takes it upon themselves to tell me I missed the mark somehow. And usually, their unsolicited opinion isn't coming from a constructive place. If it was, I could accept it, but some folks just want to make you feel like you didn't do something extraordinary, even when you clearly did.

The secret I've learned to celebrate my accomplishments is to find the value in what I've done independent of anyone else's opinion. I often tell myself, *you are a dope rapper, great speaker, amazing writer, and incredible father*. I say these things to myself on a regular basis and don't wait for someone else's validation. Then, when other people observe these qualities in me, they are merely the frosting on the cake because I see the value in who I am without seeking outside validation.

This is a superpower you must develop, especially if you hope to accomplish great things. The ability to affirm who you are and what you do regardless of others' opinions will enable you to climb to unbelievable heights. This boils down to finding a deeper purpose in your work, deeper than just trying to impress people. Make impressing yourself the focus and you'll naturally impress others. Being impressed by yourself builds a solid foundation that will keep you from doing dumb shit just for clout.

It's also interesting to note that people will have the most opinions about you when you reach a certain measure of success. People will come out of the woodworks to give you advice when they haven't done anything close to what you have and did not make any sacrifices for you to help you get where you are at. As hard as it may be, ignore them. If you feel confident in the formula you have developed for your continued growth and success, if you have a compelling vision, continue to follow those. Your success journey is unique to you. And while you may be able to emulate some people, it can only be through the lens of your own experience that you implement the practice of others. Sometimes, it's a blessing in disguise to have no blueprint to follow or guidance that you can seek. When this is the case, people cannot shape you into their image and you can truly stand as your own person, a one-of-one, a magnificent masterpiece that can never be duplicated.

I firmly believe you should be your own biggest fan, regardless of anyone else clapping for you or not. As human beings, it's virtually impossible for us not to care about what other people think of us, but you don't have to let what they think about you be the key driver in how you move through the world and make decisions. It is gratifying to make decisions and do things because they are true to you, and even more gratifying when those decisions organically resonate with other people. That's that dopest feeling in the world. But the most rewarding feeling is when you feel happy and accomplished with yourself without needing affirmation from other people to feel that way. That is true power.

I'm teaching people who come to my Gladiator School how to think more highly of themselves and sustain that belief system. Trust me, it does not happen overnight. But as your success ratio increases in different areas of life, and as you couple that with staying focused on your purpose, you can become an unstoppable force in virtually every area of life. I used to be so consumed with not wanting to self-sabotage that I attracted things into my life that could cause me to self sabotage. When I switched my mind to mainly focus on what I wanted to happen and where I wanted to go, maintaining the high level of regular success that I wanted and enjoy became easier.

It's one thing to obtain success in a moment, it's entirely different to

make it a lifestyle. And when I speak
of success, I define it as being able
to make forward progress, no matter
how small that progress may seem.
Smaller successes lead to larger ones
and allow you to scale beyond what
you think is possible from where you
currently are. That's the level I want
to get *you* to.

So, once you begin to realize a
significant level of success, when
you see real traction, I want you to
stay focused. Stay focused on your
larger purpose, which is to impact
lives and leave a mark on this world
that inspires the people around you
and those who come after you. Don't
let people diminish your success and
don't compare yourself to others. Use
others as a reference point, only as
necessary, but keep your vision on
your unique path. Stay true to that.

Demitri sat in the parking lot of the Lusty Lounge, absorbing the words he heard from Sharp Skills. He felt an uneasiness overcome him.

"Why am I even here?" He said out loud. "Everything is going well, even better than what I expected. People are actually coming to my shows and I'm making decent money. My trajectory will only go up if I stay consistent, focused, and committed to the goals I already set."

As soon as he said this, he got a text from Rich. "WYA???"

Demitri thought about his response. "Hey Rich, I appreciate you for taking an interest in my music. I gave it some more thought and I think I'm just gonna keep hammering on the path I'm on right now. I feel like it yielded some positive results and I want to see what else I can do independently."

There was no response from Rich. Demitri sat in anticipation of Rich's rebuttal, but none came. He backed out of his parking spot and headed back home. He made the decision while driving that he was going to attend Gladiator School. He needed to be in a community of like-minded people.

# FAKE FRIENDS

I need to win this contract so I can start helping put my friends into position, that way they can become just as successful as me," Kelli said as she spoke into her phone's recording app.

She liked to capture her thoughts this way, especially in moments when she was highly inspired. Kelli was a successful entrepreneur who'd built her project management consultancy into a seven-figure empire. She was also a savvy real estate investor and she had made some sound investments in distressed properties on a side of town that was the hottest up-and-coming area in her region. These investments had tripled in value within a three-year time span and boosted her net worth substantially. Not to mention, her project management firm was one of the most sought after in the country.

The goals she had put on her vision board over five years ago were manifesting right before her eyes. In the midst of all her success, Kelli felt a tinge of guilt that she couldn't shake. She couldn't understand why she felt this way, considering she was a woman of integrity and she was honest in her business affairs. Her coping mechanism was to try to shake off the guilt and find ways to give back to her community. She had already been doing so for several years prior to becoming wealthy.

Besides her guilt, what was on her mind the most these days was a new contract she was bidding on. It was the largest she had ever gone after. If her firm won this eight-figure contract, she knew she would be able to help uplift her friends and family so they could enjoy some of the success she did. This contract took up so much of her mental real estate that she hadn't even allowed herself to reflect on the fact that she was about to receive the prestigious Business Woman of the Year award at her chamber of commerce award banquet later that night.

She hit the stop recording button on her phone and proceeded with putting on her makeup and getting dressed. She slid into her well-fitted black Saint Luarent dress and Chanel pumps that had two gold c's near the toe. She put on her diamond earrings and matching necklace.

"I need to be present in this moment and celebrate this huge milestone in my life," she said to herself. She decided to focus on the award she was about to receive. She began to practice her acceptance speech:

"Thank you to the chamber for this great honor. It certainly has not been an easy road. I'd like to thank my fiance, Carter, for being my rock as I have pursued my dream of entrepreneurship. Thank you, baby. I'd like to thank my friends and family for being here tonight. You have been my support system through all of the ups and downs of my entrepreneurial journey. I'd like to thank my business partners and employees, who are like family to me. I'm so glad we are in this together. I am grateful to my clients who gave me a shot and entrusted my company with leading their projects. I hope we can work together forever."

She paused to think about who else she needed to acknowledge. Carter came out of their luxury walk-in closet, dressed in an expensive black suit, black shirt, and tie with a gold clip.

"You about ready to go, babe? We don't want to be late for your big night," he said as he grabbed her by the waist and gave her a kiss on the lips.

"Almost, my love, just putting the finishing touches on my face." She smiled at him.

"Alright cool."

He proceeded to the living room. She guessed he was going to catch up on the latest episode of his favorite show, *It Is What It Is,* hosted by Cam'ron and Ma$e. Sure enough, she heard the hosts' voices playing from the living room. She knew the special guest on this episode was Philip "Sharp Skills" Jacobs. Carter cranked up the volume on their massive flatscreen TV. Kelli could overhear it from the bedroom. As she put on the last touches of her makeup, she received several text message notifications. The group text thread between her and her seven closest friends was blowing up.

Christie

Hey girl, sorry I won't be able to attend tonight. An emergency came up and I have to handle it.

Bridgette

Ooh, I forgot about your event tonight, so sorry Kel. I'm sure there will be another moment I can celebrate with you. You have so many, it's hard to keep up lol!

Kel, I couldn't get a sitter for tonight. The nanny is on vacation. Sorry, babe

Lacey

I'm feeling a little under the weather, Kelli. I'm trying to nip this lil cold in the bud so I can make it to Misty's baby shower tomorrow. You coming to that, right? If so, I'll see you there if I'm able to shake this bug!

Kelli felt anger surge through her body. She had told her friends about this event months in advance. They knew how much she wanted them there. But they were doing what they typically do: leaving her hanging out to dry just before an event. She thought about how she consistently showed up for them during their special moments. It was an extremely rare occasion for her to not make time to support them in their endeavors.

She reflected on how she was always looking for opportunities to include her friends in lucrative business deals she was a part of or opportunities she knew about, but how they never seemed to return the favor. She consoled herself over the years by saying to herself, *God has blessed me to be a blessing, and my blessings come from Him, anyway. He sees me.* Still, her friends' lack of reciprocity had been wounding her for years, and tonight, the emotional toll felt unbearable.

"I can't believe these bitches!" she said to herself as she shook her head.

Another text came in soon after.

Misty

I'll be there, girl. I wouldn't miss this moment for the world.

A tear rolled down Kelli's cheek. Misty was seven months pregnant. She had more excuse than anyone not to show up, but here she was, putting her love into action for her friend. This gave Kelli the strength she needed to gather herself up and try to refocus her mind on the positive. She replied to the group chat.

> Kelli
>
> Thanks for the heads up, ya'll. I can't front, I'm a little disappointed you can't make it. But I understand. Life happens. See you there, Misty.

She sat down on the bed for a second to try to recenter. She keyed-in on the Philip "Sharp Skills" Jacobs interview.

                        CAM'RON
        Alright, ya'll we got a special guest
        here with us today. I've been watching
        the dude's moves from afar and must
        say, I've been quite impressed. Harlem
        niggas don't impress easily, so that's
        really saying something.

                         MA$E
        Big facts, Killa. Sharp been in
        motion. Looking forward to this convo.

                        CAM'RON
        So, y'all know our show is all about
        sports culture and Sharp has been
        doing something real unique. He's
        not an athlete but he found a way to
        build a program many elite athletes
        are participating in, called Gladiator
        School. We've heard some of the
        biggest stars in pro basketball and
        football shout him out in interviews

and on social media for the impact
his Gladiator School has had on their
performance. Welcome to the show,
Sharp.

SHARP SKILLS
Appreciate y'all for having me. First
off, I gotta say, I look at you guys
as legends and it's an honor to be
sitting with y'all on your platform.
This shit is hella dope, by the way.

CAM'RON
Appreciate that, my brotha. Ok, so
let's get into this. What is Gladiator
School and how did it develop?

SHARP SKILLS
Gladiator School is a philosophy that
came to me during one of the darkest
periods of my life. It's a program
based on all the aspects of wellness
and principles of success I use in my
life to see me through tough times.
When life got particularly hard a few
years ago, I channeled my anger and
emotion into something productive.
I got hyper-focused on working out
and building my physique, taking care
of my mental health, building my
business, going crazy in the booth...

MA$E
Yeah boy, your pen game is nice.

SHARP SKILLS
Thanks bro, that is a huge compliment
coming from an elite lyricist such as
yourself. Back to what I was saying,
going through that dark time enabled

me to create from an incredibly pure
and raw place, which I think has
contributed to excelling in my music
and all other areas of my life. What's
a trip, though, is I had to give
myself permission to be as transparent
as I have through my music, books, and
other methods of communicating with my
core audience. That took time, and it
wasn't without cost. I lost a lot of
friends through the process, or should
I say, people who were never really
friends.

CAM'RON
Say more about that. I can definitely
relate. As you grow in your success
and define yourself you lose people in
the process.

SHARP SKILLS
Facts, Cam. I think for me, and this
is something Ma$e can probably relate
to with his previous history as a
pastor, when I first started rapping
professionally, I was doing Christian
rap. And back then, I was creating
that type of music from a pure place.
But as I grew as a man and gained more
life experience, I realized I didn't
want to stay in that box. And as a
matter of fact, I couldn't, even if
I wanted to. The life experiences I
was gaining were too real for me to
sugarcoat them in my music or make
them family-friendly to appease church
people.

Definitely no shade to people in the church. I still attend myself. But I know my content now just doesn't fly there. And I don't need it to. My audience is my audience, and it's bigger than just the connections I hold in the church. With all that said, I grew apart from many people who I had connected with in the Christian rap scene because of my new creative direction and who I was becoming. I never gave up my faith in Christ, though. It's just that now my expression of that faith is drastically different.

                    MA$E
That's real honest man. I can feel that. How did you handle losing those relationships and friendships as a result of your shift in direction?

                 SHARP SKILLS
I had to look at those relationships for what they were. They were not forever friendships, meaning relationships with people who were meant to be in my life for the long haul. They were there to serve a purpose for the season of life I was in, and vice versa. And, some people I considered real friends didn't reach out to me when I was going through that dark period I mentioned earlier. Perhaps they didn't know I was going through that, or maybe they didn't care because I seemed to have changed so much. I'm not sure what the reason was. But now, at this point, it

doesn't matter. I've become so solid
in who I am that I don't need someone
who didn't stay. There's a quote by TD
Jakes that I love. He says, 'those who
are meant to be in your life, can't
leave. And those who are not meant to
be in your life, can't stay.'

CAM'RON
That's a fucking fact, Sharp. You
got me wanting to go down a rabbit
hole. Pause. In terms of friendships,
as you have come into your own as a
businessman, a brand, emcee, etc.,
how are you seeing your friendships
evolve, in general?

SHARP SKILLS
I've learned to reciprocate whatever
level of investment I see those
in my circle make toward me. It's
an adaptation I was forced to make
for my own mental health and well
being. If someone invests little,
I invest little, maybe even less.
If they invest more, I mirror that.
In the past, I was gung ho about
energetically pouring into people,
many of whom were not deserving of
that type of investment. I had to
learn the hard way because I can
be loyal to a fault sometimes. But
going through my divorce sobered me
up completely. I still extend trust
and love, but I do so with caution
now, and people have to earn greater
amounts of it from me. That's not to
say I'm demanding this from them, but
I watch patterns so I can measure

where they fall on my love and trust spectrum. These are the types of things I go into great length about in the Gladiator School sessions. I help people recognize real friends from fake ones and also friendships that have run their course.

I'm sure both of you have experienced friendships in which you simply grow apart. It's no one's fault. Like the name of your show, *It Is What It Is*. Sometimes people don't have the capacity to match your level of investment. And while you shouldn't just throw people away, you can't suffer and sacrifice yourself over and over again trying to get something you need out of that friendship, relationship, or whatever other type of connection it is, either.

You also can't waste time trying to figure out where, when, or how things may have changed in friendships or other types of relationships. You will not find closure if people are unwilling to communicate with you. Everybody can't continue with you on your journey, especially when you are trying to evolve and expand. And that's okay. It doesn't always feel good, but it is something I've learned to accept.

Unfortunately, the people who support you and rock with you in the beginning may not be the ones standing at the finish line with you. You feel me?

                    CAM'RON
     I can definitely relate to that!
     Sometimes for your own survival, you
     gotta let people go. Like, I can't
     drown tryna save you. I can't help you
     more than you want to help yourself.
     And I can't help you if you are
     willing to kill me in the process.

                    MA$E
     Damn right!


Kelli sat on the bed for a while longer after listening to the show. She felt deep in her core that she needed to hear that interview so she could decide how to move forward in her relationships with her current circle. She could relate to being loyal to a fault, and this was evidenced in the ways she made excuses for her "friends" when they didn't come through for her the way she came through for them. She knew she needed to toughen up a little more in this area without losing her tender heart in the process. She came out of the room after she put the finishing touches on her makeup.

"I'm ready to go babe," she said to Carter.

Later, when they arrived at the awards banquet, Misty was one of the first people they bumped into. Her pregnancy clearly showed, yet she was still energetic and excited to celebrate her friend during Kelli's special moment. Misty and Kelli embraced and Misty's loving spirit made her forget about how Kelli's other friends didn't seem to support her.

The three of them were escorted to the front row, near the stage. Kelli and Carter made small talk with a few of the other attendees. Still, Kelli kept looking around hoping to see some of her other friends and family unexpectedly show up. Carter caught sight of Kelli's mom and dad waiting at the entrance and he got up to go get them.

When they came over, Kelli's dad said, "I'm so proud of you, babygirl! " and he gave her a huge hug.

Her mom said, "I'm so happy to share this moment with you, K bug," trying to hold back tears of joy.

The lights dimmed and the awards banquet officially began.

# LAZINESS AND PROCRASTINATION

I'm sick of this shit!" Donovan yelled as he saw another one of his brilliant ideas launched on social media by one of the acquaintances in his social circle. This was the third time in the past two years that soon after he'd shared a game-changing idea he conceptualized in his network, someone took the ball and ran with it. Donovan had a bad habit of sharing his brilliance without following through on it, and it had cost him millions of dollars, opportunity, recognition, and prestige.

He slammed his phone down on his plush, king-sized bed. He had done alright for himself financially by establishing a career in cyber security at a top tier firm in the cyber security industry. However, he felt stuck. He couldn't seem to move up the corporate ladder at the pace he wanted, and he had incredible ideas that led him to believe he was capable of so much more than the $110K salary he earned. That $110K didn't stretch far in the major metropolitan city he lived and worked in.

The idea Donovan had shared at his last networking event was to create a cyber security device that everyday people could connect to their computers. This device would essentially act as a forcefield against evolving cyber attacks initiated by artificial intelligence. He started working on the prototype three years ago but didn't complete it due to various life circumstances and distraction. Also, he had to admit, because he was comfortable enough with his current salary, he didn't feel the pressure to finish the prototype. However, he talked about the prototype often, to anyone who would listen. Winston Jones, a colleague in his networking group and a serial entrepreneur, took special interest in Donovan's idea. During the past several networking meetups, he would ask Donovan about the progress of his idea and Donovan would spill all the beans. Winston did not have the background in cyber security Donovan did, but he knew a lucrative idea when he heard one, had the ability to raise capital and put together the team to make things happen, and he had a relentless drive to complete things he started.

Donovan didn't know all this at the time, and he failed to have his business affairs in order to protect his ideas. When he saw Winston's well-polished infomercial about the Neutralizer of Artificial Intelligence Threat (NAIT), he had to stop himself from vomiting. What's worse, Winston had gained several thousand likes and followers because of the NAIT. Comments such as, "Wow! This is a brilliant idea. You are a genius, Winston!" and "What I would give to have a mind like yours. Wish I'd thought of that," infuriated Donovan.

Donovan sat in his leather chair brooding for the rest of the day and evening. He even had a brief thought of killing Winston with the NAIT. The thought of bashing Winston's face in with the NAIT like it was a rock brought a smile to his face. Luckily, he snapped out of that dark rumination. He knew he wasn't built for prison. He lingered in deep thought, thinking about all sorts of things, like what was he going to do with his life. He knew his current occupation wasn't fulfilling to him anymore, especially when his ideas were making other people rich. He thought about how procrastination and downright laziness in the form of comfortable complacency was costing him the life he dreamed about. A life where he could make a real difference, be his own boss, come and go as he pleased, and in which money was not an issue. At 42 years old, he began to think that maybe it was too late for him to realize his dreams. Maybe where he currently was in life was all that was meant for him. Or was it?

He scanned the vast collection of books in his library. Many had gone unread. He locked eyes on two in particular, *Accuracy: Hit Your Mark in Life* and *You Are the Solution*. Both were written by Philip "Sharp Skills" Jacobs. Out of all his books, these titles stood out to him for some mysterious reason. He got out of his chair, stretched a little bit, and went to grab them off the shelf. He opened *Accuracy* and scanned the table of contents to see if anything resonated.

*Chapter 8: Occupation*, stood out to him. He turned to it and looked at the segments inside. *Work Ethic* on page 151 grabbed his attention. He began to read it out loud.

## Work Ethic

You may have heard the witty saying, "The only time success comes before work is in the dictionary." These are words to live by as it relates to occupation. Our road to accuracy in the vocational environment is our strong work ethic. Your commitment to give your best every day is what will set you apart in your endeavors and ultimately lead to your success. It's funny how the simplest truths regarding success are ignored. It is human nature to travel the road of least resistance. In other words, it's inherent for all of us to be lazy.

So many people give into this destructive trait by cloaking it with the mask of busyness. Now, more than ever it is easy to give our attention to everything except what we should focus our energies on. It's much easier to feel productive than to actually be productive. Hard work is, well, hard. Part of that hard work nowadays is related to staying focused and not giving into the gravitational pull of surface level productivity.

We must be willing to consistently invest our time, energy, mental capacity and even our financial resources into what we are pursuing. There are several different factors that contribute to vocational success, but work ethic is the granddaddy of them all. Every position that I've done well in could be traced back to the launching pad called "the grind." Your drive is what will generate your desired result. The time in which we live does not promote this line of thinking. It often seems that the spin of today's media is to focus our attention on the one in a million or the meteoric rise of someone famous. This produces a false notion that success comes easily. We see people who seemingly have equal or lesser talent than us on larger platforms. All the while, we are not aware of what put that person in their current position.

Accuracy teaches us that our fortunes lie buried under the timeless principles of determination, perseverance, focus, and work. Accurate lives work hard on the things that matter and tend to brush off the things that glitter but are far from gold. I am inspired by the work ethic of many entrepreneurs that I have witnessed in the Korean-American community. I've been in several of their family owned businesses and have seen every employee pour their best effort into whatever assignment they are given. The CEOs and presidents of these companies are typically the hardest workers in their firms.

I was intrigued by the work ethic of the Korean-Americans whom I had encountered so I began to do a little research on how they developed it. It turns out that many of the first-generation Korean-Americans came to the United States in hope for a better life but could not find work or were forced to do back-breaking labor that paid below minimum wage. In order to overcome this, many became entrepreneurs in order to provide a good life for their children and grandkids. They place a high value on education and many Korean-American parents work strenuous hours in order to fund their children's education. I also discovered that the racism and other obstacles they faced in this country caused them to remain a tight-knit community in support for one another. You often see Korea towns or entire business districts dominated by these resilient people.

I once went into a fast food restaurant that was owned by a Korean-American woman and she worked harder than all of her staff. She did everything from working the cash register, to cooking the fries, to greeting guests, and brining their food to them. I was impressed by her work ethic. On top of that, she worked 12 hours a day, seven days a week. I'm not necessarily suggesting we all adopt that same schedule and work routine, but there is something to glean from this young woman. She has a "by any means necessary" attitude to succeed in her occupation, and she has really taken her future into her own hands by buying a business and working it.

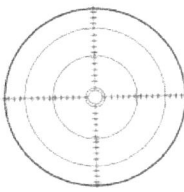

## Scope of Accuracy – South Korea

*South Korea is a country with a rich legacy. The struggles that Koreans have faced and overcome has instilled in them a work ethic and drive for excellence that is unparalleled. The country suffered devastation after the Korean War and one-third of the population became homeless. However, the*

Donovan contemplated his work ethic and how he needed to improve it if he wanted to rise above his current life status. In *Accuracy*, one part resonated deeply with him.

*"Accuracy teaches us that our fortunes lie buried under the timeless principles of determination, perseverance, focus, and work. Accurate lives work hard on the things that matter and tend to brush off the things that glitter but are far from gold.*

What this meant to him was that he needed to find a way to eradicate the distractions that easily took him off-track from his work and apply as much of his focus as he possibly could toward his desired outcomes.

After he wrote this thought down in a notebook, he opened *You Are the Solution* and looked through the chapters to see what stood out to him in relation to his current situation. He settled on Chapter 8.

*Chapter 8: Execute Like Your Life Depends On It.*

It wasn't lost on him that both chapters were Chapter 8. He recalled that the number 8 represents new beginnings. And, he felt like that was exactly what he needed. A new beginning. He flipped to page 134 and began to read aloud again.

You want productivity to become a habit, not a sporadic event. If you want to produce something meaningful, you must train yourself to be consistent when you aren't feeling it. The difference separating the extraordinary from average people is they simply won't give up. They are relentless. You have to wake up every day and tell yourself in the mirror, "I'm an executer! I will be productive today." If you set this tone for your life through positive affirmations, eventually your emotions will follow suit. You won't feel like going to the gym until after you start working out. You won't feel like doing that research paper until you start reading the scholarly articles that point to fascinating conclusions. You won't feel like

feeding those suffering from homelessness until you get out in the community and start handing out meals. Our energy will shift, and we will start to *feel* like executing once we *do* something.

The rare instances when we are motivated before we start something are inconsistent and won't help us complete anything substantial if we rely too heavily on them. It's better to use those moments as wind in our sails as we continue the daily grind of paddling. You have no control over when the wind will pick up, however, you can control how you take advantage of the wind when it comes your way. Other than that, you better get to rowing if you hope to make it to your desired destination!

He reflected on this portion for a moment.

*If you want to produce something meaningful, you must train yourself to be consistent when you aren't feeling it. The difference separating the extraordinary from average people is they simply won't give up. They are relentless.*

This made him think about all the times he started projects but didn't complete them due to life issues arising. Some of these issues were so small he could've got right back to working on his projects or continuing to work on them in their midst. He was upset with himself for not having this mindset and he wasn't sure if he could change. But then he repeated the mantra in the book forcefully.

"*I'm an executor! I will be productive today.*"

He said it over and over again, getting louder each time until he got emotional. He began to cry as he continued saying it, each time with more passion. He felt something inside him shifting, and he had a vision of what it would look and feel like to accomplish his dreams. He stood up and walked to his bathroom mirror and stared at himself intensely. He looked at the gray hairs on his scalp starting to multiply. And although he still looked fairly young for his age, he saw how his face was showing signs of aging. He realized he was not a young man anymore and he needed to stop making excuses about why he wasn't where he wanted to be in life.

It was then and there that he vowed to pour himself into his vision. He wasn't going to let anything or anyone stop him. This may be the last shot he had to truly make something of himself, something he could be proud of and that lived up to his potential. With this newfound belief system in place, he went to his office and began to put together a schedule for his newest idea. He jotted down thoughts on how to creatively market it to potential customers. He knew if his NAIT idea could work, he could come up with something else, potentially something even better. He put on his calendar that he would dedicate at least two hours every day to working on his idea until it was finished. He wrote out an entire process for how he was going to realize his vision and the things he thought he needed to get there.

He wrote his goal in the middle of the paper and circled it: Multi AI Platform Bridge (MAP Bridge)

- Begin trademark/patent and additional research to see if the idea already exists
- If the idea doesn't exists, register website domain name
- Prepare data
- Decide on best tools to use for this project
- Design AI app
- Test and fine tune
- Let TRUSTED friends and family who sign an NDA (non disclosure agreement) test the application
- Refine app based on feedback
- Contact Sheryl Jones for marketing strategy advice
- Soft launch of app at upcoming International Conference on Machine Learning...

As he wrote this process out, he felt more empowered than he had in years. He knew he was onto something, he just needed to stay consistent. That was where the true test was. After he finished, he Googled Philip "Sharp Skills" Jacobs to see what the author had been up to since writing these transformative books. He found Sharp Skills' website and saw an informational video about something called Gladiator School. After watching it, Donovan knew he needed to be there. He needed to be around other people who were building their capacity to be resilient and productive. He pulled out his credit card and immediately signed up for the workshop experience.

# BUSY AND OVERWHELMED

Leilani slapped her forehead in frustration as she received another email from her son's football team asking her to grab snacks... again. This was the third time in a row this month that she'd been asked to provide the aftergame snacks. The other parents never volunteered to carry some of the load.

This wasn't the only reason she was frustrated, though. She was the director of a large non-profit and it felt like the same thing happening with her son's football team was taking place at work. Although she had a staff of 12 people, it seemed like she was responsible for planning all the organizational events while also running the day-to-day operations. When she asked for help, people tended to brush her off because she had a way of always pulling things together and making it look easy.

Leilani also sat on boards for two different organizations. Her board service started as a way for her to give back to her community, but it always turned into the "Leilani's got this" show. She was often called upon to organize major fundraising events for both organizations. Leilani was a gifted organizer, planner, and executor who tended to thrive when she had several projects going, but her mental health was starting to suffer. She was finding it hard to remember things and wasn't spending the amount of time she wanted to with her son. As a single mom, she felt like her son was spending more time with her mother than his actual mother because of how busy Leilani was. Nowadays, she also found herself complaining a lot more and being sharp with people, though she tended to be happy, lighthearted and courteous.

She messaged the team email. "I guess I can do it again this week, too."

She hoped someone would pick up on how burdened she felt. But one of the coaches just responded, "Great. Please pick up something different this week because the kids are complaining that the snacks are all the same. Appreciate it."

Leliani was livid when she saw this thoughtless response, but she didn't give-in to it. Plus, she felt like part of her bonding time with her son took place through football. She grabbed her keys to head to the store to pick up the snacks. Before she left the house, she got a call from her best friend, Sonjay. She planned to call her back when she got home from the store, but Sonjay called her again. Thinking it was an emergency, Leilani fumbled to grab her phone and answered.

"Hey girl, are you ok?"

"Yeah, I'm fine. Just wanted to see what you are doing this weekend. I got tickets to the Sharp Skills concert and I want you to come. The seats are really good."

"I wish I could, girl, but I got so much on my plate, I don't think I'm going to be able to."

"Dang, okay. You are always working so hard. You deserve to live a little. But I get it, let me know if you change your mind. But I need to know within the next day or so. These tickets are selling out quickly."

"Will do. I'll keep you posted."

They hung up. As Leilani drove to the store, she thought more and more about what Sonjay said and she knew her friend was right. She needed to live a little and let her hair down or she was going to go crazy.

When she arrived at the store, she grabbed a credit card she had been keeping in her glovebox solely for emergencies. She had been doing well, not using it unless she needed to. But without giving herself a chance to talk herself out of it, she grabbed the card and moved like a woman on a mission toward the large warehouse store. She filled her basket with almost whatever she feasted her eyes on that she had been wanting; a new bluetooth speaker, laptop, a new watch, designer cookware, clothes, and she placed an order for a new leather massage chair. By the time she got to the register to check out, her basket was filled to the brim. People were staring at her, but she ignored them, feeling completely justified.

"Your total today is $8,741.45 mam," the cashier said.

She whipped out her credit card and swiped quickly. She then decisively walked out of the store before she gave herself time to return anything. When she got to the car, her common sense came back. She knew she needed to do something to help herself so she wouldn't let her overspending get to this point again. She texted Sonjay.

"I think I'm going to take you up on that offer to go to the Sharp Skills concert. I really need it."

Sonjay immediately texted back a heart emoji.

Leilani had butterflies in her stomach as she rode in the car with Sonjay to the concert. It had been a while since she had dolled herself up and stepped out for a night on the town. She wore a tight-fitting leather suit with gold zippers and high heel leather pumps with gold bottoms. When she dressed up, she did it well. Leilani was enjoying listening to the loud music while her long, jet black hair blew in the wind in Sonjay's dark purple, Chevy Camaro convertible.

Leilani promised herself she was going to enjoy herself tonight and not worry about anything else. They arrived at a packed Tacoma Dome, where thousands of Sharp Skills fans were waiting their turn to either park or get into the venue. They finally found a spot, Sonjay paid for the parking, and then they headed inside. The tickets were great. They were only seven rows back from the stage.

After sitting for 20 minutes waiting for the concert to start, Leilani's anxiety started to kick in. She thought about all the things she needed to do tomorrow. She also thought about what her son was doing and if he was okay.

Sonjay was incredibly intuitive and could feel her friend drifting away mentally. She had also attended one of Sharp Skills' Gladiator School sessions a year ago and learned how to be more present in the moment. She rubbed Leilani on the arm.

"Stay with me girl. I can tell you overthinking some shit right now."

Leilani looked at her with a mix of irritation and appreciation in her eyes, she knew her friend was right.

"Don't be acting like you know me," she retorted sarcastically. They both laughed.

Then suddenly, the lights dimmed in the arena and videos of Sharp Skills began to play on the large screens while his music played on full blast. The crowd was mesmerized by the presentation. About four minutes in, everything stopped, the spotlight hit the stage and he ran out and stood tall and proud. The crowd went wild. Leilani forgot about her troubles and was immersed in the show.

"What up, Rebels!" Sharp Skills said with passionate force as he waited on a response from the crowd.

Everyone, including Leilani, lost it again and yelled back. Sharp then performed song after song flawlessly. His band was out of this world. He weaved powerful messages into his music throughout his performance to uplift the people.

"Before I get to this next song, I wanted to share something that's on my heart," he said.

"Get it, Sharp!" someone from the crowd yelled.

"I know some of y'all had to push through some bullshit to get here tonight. Whether that be pressure from work, school, family, or just life. I know it can be heavy, even unbearable at times, to deal with all that pressure. And people with big hearts... we tend to have it the worst. Because as much we wanna act like we don't give a fuck, we do. It's hard for us to not be invested in the things and people we are associated with. Because of this, we take on more weight than we should. This also creates false expectations in those around us, because when we've carried ourselves like superheroes for so long, people don't understand it when we finally act human. I don't know who needs to hear this right now, but it's ok to be human. Matter of fact, you have to be human. It's cool to be a superhero sometimes, but even Superman has to revert back to Clark Kent at a certain point.

Some of y'all might be thinking, *isn't this the dude who wrote* Gladiator? *Isn't that meant to help us be stronger mentally?* And my response to that is, yes to both questions. That said, I understand that no one can be a true gladiator if they are carrying things that don't belong to them for an extended period of time. Gladiators have to learn which responsibilities are theirs to shoulder and which ones they have to let go of. Otherwise, they risk death. Not always physically, but mentally and spiritually. As a gladiator, you have to be clear about what your purpose is, and what is yours to own as you move through different phases of life. You have to know what dead weight to cut or even some of the so-called good things, you feel me?

Sometimes we can make the mistake of carrying a certain weight because subconsciously, we are trying to prove to others (and ourselves) that we are worthy of love and acceptance. Life and toxic people have a way of trying to impress upon your mind that you are not enough and you always have to jump through hoops, do more, and carry more, if you want access to the good that life has to offer. I say fuck that!"

The crowd yelled in agreement.

"Don't get me wrong, I am all for hard and productive work. And for taking responsibility for the things that belong to me in my life. I'm even down to help lighten the load for family and friends when they are in a jam. But I'm not for doing these things because I have to prove something in order to be accepted. I've done that before and now, the new me, the gladiator, will buck against that every time.

I'm already more than enough. I accept myself, regardless of who doesn't. And all the dope shit I do in life, whether it's being a great father, a sharp businessman, or a world class artist, I now understand is only a byproduct of my essence. This shift in mindset has not only opened an abundance of new opportunities to me, it has endowed me with incredible self-peace. And if you haven't noticed, peace is a rare state of being in the world today.

So friends, my fellow Rebels, I just want to encourage y'all to accept yourselves today. Don't let yourself get busy and overwhelmed with things that are not your responsibility. And if you are overwhelmed by things that are your responsibility, allow yourself to be human. Take the cape off for a moment. I promise you it's not going anywhere. You *are* a superhero and that identity isn't going to cease to exist. But allow yourself to be real, to say from time to time,

'I don't have things together the way I want them to be. It's hard as hell spinning all these plates. Every now and then, some of those plates are going to drop and crack. And you know what, that's cool. Life goes on.'

You will learn lessons from those broken plates and figure out how to spin them more efficiently in the future, or realize you didn't have no business spinning all of those damn plates in the first place. Ok, rant done. Let's get back to the music now! Band, let's gooooo!"

Sharp launched into one of his biggest hits, "Catch A Vibe."

*I'm just tryna catch a vibe,*
*thanking God for everyday that I'm alive,*
*billion dollar thoughts on mind,*
*the pains for perspective when we shine,*
*staying humble when I make it to the top...*

The crowd went into pandemonium, singing word for word.

Leilani treasured Sharp's words in her heart, thinking about which plates she needed to keep spinning, which ones she should drop, and which plates she would no longer spin in the future. It deeply resonated with her that she had to give herself permission to be human and remove the superhero cape regularly. Also, she needed to let other people know when she was taking it off.

She was also intrigued to learn more about what it took for Sharp to become a true gladiator. She wanted to learn how to grow into one, too. But for now, she was just going to enjoy the rest of the show, with her cape off.

# WELCOME TO GLADIATOR SCHOOL

**B**rian fidgeted in his chair a little in excitement of the first day of Gladiator School, which was starting within the next ten minutes. He looked around the large industrial compound he was in. It had wall-length murals of inspiring figures such as Kobe Bryant, Muhammed Ali, Serena Williams, Nipsey Hussle, Malcolm X, and other prominent social figures. The compound had the feel of a small military base, but also the charm of a luxury resort. Every area seemed to be laid out with great thought and aesthetic. In one corner of the space was what appeared to be a combat zone with a mixed martial arts ring, several punching bags, hitting pads, swords, knives, spears, bows, arrows, long black sticks and various types of body armor that looked like modern day samurai attire. Not far from that was an enclosed gun range with several rifles and pistols hanging from a display wall. Across from the interior gun range was a significant library with books all the way up to the 25-foot ceiling. There were plush gold and black couches, matching tables, and quiet study areas inside it. Adjacent to that was a fitness area with free weights, weight benches, peloton bikes, stairmasters, workout machines, medicine balls, and a sauna. The ground floor of the compound, which housed all of this, looked like a James Bond movie set.

Brian looked up, realizing there was also an upstairs level. He saw a huge recording studio, a creative space with arts supplies, and what he thought might be a movie theater. The Rebel Firm logo was emblazoned on the middle of the ceiling and floor, for all to see.

Brian's 13 other Gladiator School attendees sat and chatted in an equally perceptible anticipation and excitement of what was to come. The large digital timer in front of them counted down, *five, four, three, two, one…* and finally, out came Philip "Sharp Skills" Jacobs from a side door with a half dozen of his staff members. They all wore black Rebel Firm sweat suits with red embroidery across the chest. Sharp Skills stood front and center of the Gladiator School attendees with a reserved posture but a lighthearted grin on his face. One by one, he made eye contact with the attendees with a piercing intensity. Brian knew they were about to begin a journey that could shape the course of the rest of their lives.

"Welcome to Gladiator School, folks. I've led several sessions like this and it never ceases to amaze me that I feel the gravity of the moment every time," said Sharp Skills. "That's because I've been where many of you are at one point or another in my life. I've had to face demons and conquer them. I know what it feels like to feel alone, lost, and even powerless. But somehow, each and every one of you mustered up the courage and grit to get here today, refusing to let life just keep happening to you. And for that, you should be proud of yourselves.

You all came here looking for something and only you can find it. My staff and I will be your supportive guides along the way, but it is your personal intention that will help you obtain what you seek. Gladiator School is about doing the shadow work that people tend to hide from. It's all about conducting the internal soul searching work that helps you get crystal clear about who you must become to lead the type of life you want.

Over the course of the weekend, you will be invited to discover aspects of yourself you didn't know existed and you will be equipped with the mental weaponry necessary to conquer your greatest fears. Up here with me is my therapist, Rick, my mixed martial arts trainer, Tim, my personal fitness trainer, Martin, my financial advisor, Kenny, my spiritual advisor, TD Jakes, and my attorney, Lindsey. This is the team I assembled to navigate the darkness and maximize my fullest potential, and I am sharing them with you during our time together. Let me say a few about each.

My therapist, Rick, taught me how to see life for what it was, not what I wanted it to be. This was, and still is, important for me because to make drastic changes in your life, you have to be grounded in reality. Living in a fantasy will get you nowhere. Progress is made by understanding where you are truly at.

My mixed martial arts trainer, Tim, helped turn me into a badass. Not only from the standpoint of being able to whoop somebody's ass, definitively, if the occasion ever arose, but more importantly, he's helped me develop the inner confidence to not cower in the face of life's battles. Practicing mixed martial arts has made me a much calmer person when conflict arises. One of my go-to strategies when life throws a punch at me is to breathe before I respond.

Martin, my personal trainer, has guided me on my journey of pushing past my physical limits. What started as a desire to have a "revenge body" after my divorce has evolved into a lifestyle of working out and building physical strength. This has served me well in many ways. It has given me the confidence to not settle for less in business arrangements and to not downplay my worth.

Kenny, my financial advisor, has helped me to better understand the financial markets. And while I manage the majority of my portfolio, he has provided me value in researching assets that are not already on my radar and he gives me a different perspective on what I should invest in. I recommend that everyone learn how to manage their own finances and investments, but a financial advisor can be a key asset to your gladiator team, especially if you have a desire to be wealthy.

My spiritual advisor is TD Jakes. Bishop Jakes has guided me through some very tough circumstances, providing me with wise words when I needed them most. I'm of the Christian faith, but no matter your faith tradition, I think it's critical to have someone or some resource you can listen to to gain a higher perspective than your own.

Last but certainly not least, my attorney, Lindsey, helped me navigate my divorce. She was expensive as shit, but she fought for me in ways I couldn't. She also coached me when shit got rocky post-divorce. Having a good attorney on your team is important because we all need someone who knows how to navigate the legal system, whether that be in business, family law, or even criminal justice. As a gladiator, you gotta know which battles to fight and when you need to recruit someone who is a specialist in certain forms of warfare.

This is my team. They have their own segments, which they will lead you through this weekend. Now, I want to segway into talking about this state of the art facility you are sitting in. This facility represents different phases of my journey, each of which enabled me to overcome the darkest seasons in my life. The combat and weapons area represents how I made the decision to not become a victim, but a weapon. The purpose was not to become a weapon that can hurt people, although that is a byproduct, but a weaponized mindset to slice through the bullshit life was sending my way. A weapon in the hands of a skilled warrior has the potential to not only destroy but also liberate. I needed to liberate myself from my personal demons and my past mistakes. And this combat zone is a physical representation of an internal reality.

The library represents my journey of self-discovery and a thirst to learn about life through new lenses. Learning is growing. When you expand your understanding and knowledge, you can become more. You must obtain new knowledge daily and make it a discipline you fiercely protect. That means you set boundaries, even with your loved ones, that you enforce. I view knowledge like currency. The more I build it up, the more options I have to improve my life.

The fitness area represents the ocean of sweat equity I have put into becoming someone I'm proud is looking back at me in the mirror. It represents my grind, tenacity, and grit to charge through the darkness until my inner light shines so bright that it illuminates what was once a pitch black tunnel. I believe we are the light at the end of our tunnel, but we have to uncover our light, first. And once we see the light within ourselves, we must refuse to let ourselves or others hide it. Creating a lifestyle of personal fitness gave me the foundation needed to forge through the fog until my mind became completely clear.

The final area which has great significance for our Gladiator School is the creative spaces above. Since I'm a hip hop artist, it was natural for me to build a top-notch recording studio, as it is directly tied to my inner gift. However, the studio and the creative space are also representations of a core element of my gladiator journey: I have to create! I believe we all have the potential and power to create ourselves out of any negative situation and into a much better one. Every human was endowed with the ability to create something beautiful, even if it's not deemed art by the world we live in. I argue that whatever you create, whether it be paintings or spreadsheets, you have the capacity to create breathtaking masterpieces."

Lincoln was especially energized by this part of the tour.

"One thing I want to stress before we officially begin," continued Sharp Skills, " is that even though you are all here together, much of the work you will be doing is going to be done in isolation. Becoming a gladiator is a lonely business. Most people won't understand you and if you stay the course long enough, you'll lose the desire to explain it to them. Either you are a gladiator or you're not. Life's pressures will reveal if you are, and gladiators will naturally recognize each other.

I'll bet that many of you have friends and family you haven't felt supported by even when you've fully supported them."

Misty looked down at the floor, trying to hold back her emotions. Sharp Skills was walking right down her street.

"And because of this, you've had to learn how to be your own best cheerleader. You've had to develop the skill of comforting your own soul and being your greatest ally. While it's not fun, this isolation has instilled a solidity in you that has equipped you to go to heights others around never even dreamed was possible. And that's a good thing. You are a chosen one, with a purpose to impact many lives. That always comes at the price of deep isolation. So we are going to tap into that treasure trove, enable you to understand it so you can unlock this precious gift, and no longer fear it.

Part of how we do this is teaching you how to map-out key parts of your life journey so you get a holistic view of the trajectory you've been on. Understanding these specific parts of your past will give you a clearer sense of what your future holds. Perhaps not the full picture, but certain aspects of this picture will be revealed.

Even though the bulk of Gladiator School will focus on isola-tion, one of the benefits of being here is that you are surrounded by like-minded individuals determined to build their mental toughness. There will be activities and challenges you will pursue together and make each other sharper as a result.

The first activity we are going to do together is something I haven't shown the world yet. You will be the first group to do it. By a quick show of hands, how many of you are familiar with the board game Reveal the Elephant, which I released a couple years ago?"

Most of the group raised their hands.

"Alright cool. We received such a great response from that board game from organizations and individuals who'd played it that we thought we'd gamify the journey of becoming a gladiator, as well. Reveal the Elephant has been helping millions of people and professionals have difficult conversations about race, racism, and racial equity in the workplace. Companies that have struggled to actionize their diversity, equity, inclusion, and anti-racism strategies have found a way forward with this game. I receive notes all the time from executives telling me how they have improved their workplace culture due to playing it with their teams.

When I was conceptualizing Gladiator School, I thought a great way to introduce people to this concept and help them build skills necessary for it along the way, in addition to the book, would be to create a game board experience."

Donovan lit up like a Christmas tree when he heard this idea. It inspired him as an inventor to see another innovator following through with his ideas and creating a product that would massively benefit people. He held his excitement in. He was honored to be part of the first group to play this game.

"Let me give you an overview of the Gladiator Game™," said Sharp Skills. "The purpose of the game is to level-up from victim to Gladiator, and you will do this by addressing various challenges and opportunities as you roll the dice of life. Similar to chess, you may start off as a pawn, but when you make it all the way to the other side of the board, you will become a king or queen. When you roll the dice, you will move your piece the number of spaces indicated and you will draw a prompt card either from the opportunity or challenge pile. You'll read the card aloud and answer how you will address the opportunity or challenge you are facing. For extra points, you can write out a short affirmation, or what I like to call a Statement of Intention (SOI) that pertains to the opportunity or challenge. Every element I've shared in the beginning of class today is in the boardgame. The game has special gladiator areas called the library, combat zone, gym, and creative enterprise. When you land in those areas, you will draw a Gladiator Advisor card which will share some sort of knowledge and wisdom with you. The advisor categories are Therapist, Fight Trainer, Fitness Trainer, Spiritual Guide, Financial Advisor, and Legal Counsel. For example, if you land in the combat zone, you may draw a Gladiator Advisor card that reads:

Fight Trainer

"Death is not the greatest loss in life. The greatest loss is what dies inside while still alive. Never surrender."

– Tupac Shakur


There will be all sorts of nuggets of wisdom you can gather and take with you while on the journey of playing this game. These nuggets of wisdom help players go from victims to gladiators.

Leilani blurted out, "That's dope as hell!"

Everybody laughed in agreement.

"Thanks, Leilani. My team and I have really done our best to encapsulate my journey in developing mental toughness because I believe it can resonate with so many people who desire to overcome life's challenges and seize its opportunities."

"We've got the board games set up to my right," said one of Sharp Skills' staff members. He pulled a large black covering back from a table, revealing the beautifully designed Gladiator Games.

"Before we get to the game though, I want you all to set your intention for the day and this weekend," said Sharp Skills. "You see there are various murals of great figures surrounding the space, and around those murals are hundreds of carefully curated Statements of Intention I've personally written. I was inspired to write these after I realized that what a person thinks about consistently, they eventually become. So we have to be extremely intentional about our thoughts. These SOI's have been my way to build a fortress around my mind. I only let down the drawbridge for thoughts that are in alignment with who I want to become, and they defend against the thoughts that are contrary to my intentions. My process for creating these was to simply visualize who I want to become and write statements from the perspective of that version of myself.

Our lives flow in the direction of our intentions. Through intention, we recognize things we might otherwise overlook. This principle is easiest to see in real life, like when we buy a new car. All of the sudden, we see that same car on the road all the time. Those cars similar to yours were there the whole time, but because you now have this car, which represents intent in this scenario, you can spot the car with your eyes closed.

I want you to walk around the space and find a SOI that resonates with you and which you want to make your own while you are in Gladiator School. We are going to build on the SOI that you choose. After you all have done your walkthrough and found your SOI, we'll get started. Alright, let's get to it."

Everybody got up and began to look at the various SOI's around the facility.

# STATEMENTS OF INTENTION

**B**rian's eyes were instantly drawn to an SOI about divorce. He read it to himself.

My divorce does not define my future relationships. I will learn from my mistakes in this relationship and move on with my life. All relationships run their course one way or another; it was just time for this one's expiration. It is now time to heal and focus on becoming the best version of myself. There is someone out there better for me and there is someone out there that I am better for. I will hold no grudges or resentment toward my former spouse. I lovingly release them and wish them the best. They are no longer my partner and I let them go, permanently. It is now time to heal and focus on becoming the best version of myself. I am healing and becoming the best version of myself. The ideal mate will enter my life at the right time. I am committed to taking care of my kids and providing them with the best life I possibly can. I will not let the fact that things are not working with their mother keep me from being fully present in their lives. I won't let anything come between me and my sons. I am grateful my sons and I have a great relationship and I will put forth maximum and unwavering effort to maintain it. Though I desire companionship, I am whole by myself. I don't need someone else to make me happy. I make myself happy. I am becoming the best version of myself!

Brian knew that this SOI was for him.

Tanya read through several SOI's and finally came across one she felt she could take ownership of.

My body is a magnificent wonder. I am fearfully and wonderfully made. My body operates as it should and I take excellent care of it. My body is the vehicle by which I exercise my purpose, therefore I honor it and treat it with the utmost respect. I eat healthy foods rich in nutrients that nourish me. I manage my stress well. Life's stressors do not get the best of me. I drink lots of water, I breathe deeply, I practice self care, and I do things I enjoy with people I enjoy. I am incredibly healthy in body, mind, and spirit. My strong mind sustains my strong body. My body fights against illness and bounces back quickly after injury. I am athletic and agile. I have longevity and a powerful life force inside me. I physically move like I'm half my age. I workout regularly, lift weights, and do cardio. I am excited to workout and my body responds well to it. I look good and I feel great.

Tanya touched these words on the wall and made this SOI the intention of her heart.

Lincoln had made his way upstairs. A rebel of sorts, he thought he'd use the time to get a closer look at the creative space. As he walked up, however, he caught a glance of an SOI that jumped out at him about money.

I work hard to put myself in position for money to come easily to me. My creativity allows me to manifest the life of my dreams. My artistry is well resourced and I am paid at a high premium for my brilliance. The money I make is reinvested back into my art and myself. I am a self-fulfilling prophecy of wealth and prosperity. My money earns more money and I am freely able to pursue my interests without care for money. I am financially free. I am so abundant I can easily give to others in need. I also share the game through which I learned to help others position themselves to be financially liberated. Money comes to me easily because I know what to do with it. I've created multiple streams of income and they all produce well for me. I enjoy watching my investments continue to grow. I am excited about the new opportunities to generate more wealth that are coming my way. Let's get it.

Lincoln sat down on the stairs after he read the SOI, processing and thinking about how he could make these words a reality.

Layla kept pacing around the library, contemplating the SOI she saw which had hit home for her.

I am solid in who I am. I stand on a firm foundation that allows me to expand as a person. My soul is anchored even when my mind wanders. That's natural, and I'm always able to bring my mind back to center. I know who I am, I know what I'm doing, and I know where I'm going. Even though life is constantly changing, the essence of who I am remains the same. I am discovering new aspects of my identity, but I now realize they've been there all along. I've learned how to harmonize the parts of myself I have known with the parts that are newly uncovered. I might adapt to my environment, but I don't allow it to shape me. I shape it. The pressure life puts on me is only further exposing the diamond I am. I'm strong to my core in my identity even if my paradigm shifts. I only improve, I only become better, I only manifest more inner greatness. I'm true to myself, I have deep knowledge of self and I stay real. I place boundaries around myself, I protect my peace and my authentic essence continues to thrive.

Layla's eyes welled-up with tears as she continued to repeat this SOI to herself.

Travis stood by the weight benches as he looked at the various SOI's in the gym. He came across one that resonated with him on a fundamental level.

I am a deep thinking individual with a vast amount of potential and there is so much greatness in my life. The big purpose for me that is being unveiled requires me to go through seasons of isolation. The same way seeds must be buried in the soil, where it is dark, I must go through periods of being covered and alone. I understand that times of isolation allow me to become phenomenally acquainted with myself in ways I cannot access when I'm part of the crowd. I was never made to be part of the crowd, but to impact it, to be a leader within it. All great people go through isolation and I am no different. Even though I don't like it at times, I embrace isolation and feelings of loneliness because I know it is producing the character in me needed to fulfill my purpose. It is forging my inner steel, which enables me to not bend, fold, or break from the opinions of others. I stand strong, with my back straight and my chest out in boldness, because I have gone through the fires of isolation to release my inner conqueror. In short, I'm not to be fucked with. Quote me on that!

Travis pounded his chest after reading this and knew this was his SOI.

Crystal knew instantly which SOI belonged to her. She had felt like a sponge since the moment she walked into the facility. Before she knew they were going to be doing the SOI walkthrough, she had already begun reading them throughout the day. She chose one she kept returning to during breaks.

> I adapt to all of life's circumstances. Life is not happening to me, it's happening for me. Even the most difficult life changes I face have something in them that is working toward producing a good outcome for me. I will not allow the fear of change to paralyze me. I radically accept my new reality as it is and I continue to take steps to shape my future. I am resilient and resourceful. I have everything I need to adjust and continue to thrive in an evolving landscape. I am flexible and mentally nimble. I figure out ways to win no matter what situation I find myself in. I have landed on my feet several times in the past and this pattern will continue in my present and future. I have resolved to press through no matter what life sends my way. I can do it, I will do it, I must do it.

Crystal smiled to herself and emotionally embraced her SOI. She was confident this would be a statement that would be a north star in her life for years to come.

Demitri gazed at the hundreds of statements of intent on the wall near the creative space. He read through several of them and began to piece together Philip's success journey. He recognized that it wasn't a pretty ride, but in some way, the pain Philip inadvertently expressed in his SOI statements was beautiful, especially considering the outcome. Then, one leaped off the wall at Demitri.

I am successful even before the full fruit of my labor is evident. I am a success within myself and the external outcome is only the byproduct of my inner reality. While I welcome outside validation, I don't need it. I'm already the shit and I know it. I don't need people to tell me that. I look myself in the mirror and I see the embodiment of my dreams. All external success is fleeting, it is the character that I develop on this journey that is the real prize. I'm proud of my progress no matter how others feel about it, whether that progress feels positive, negative, or neutral. I have become more so I can do more, therefore I will have more. I am more! I am more than enough. I am happy with my level of achievement even as I continue to pursue new goals and ambitions. I have created a winning formula after several years of trial and error and I won't let anyone talk me out of what I have been able to accomplish. Whether millions know about what I've done or only I do, I have manifested a magnificent life and what I've established on earth will resound throughout eternity.

After he read this, Demitri closed his eyes and imagined what extreme belief in this SOI would look like in his life.

Kelli nodded her head in disbelief as she read an SOI that pertained to her situation so accurately it felt like she wrote it herself.

I deserve great friendships and relationships where support, love, and loyalty are reciprocated. I lovingly release friendships that no longer serve me. I realize that history with people does not equate to connection. I set healthy boundaries in all my relationships and only reciprocate to the level that others invest. I am grateful for the solid friendships and relationships I have. I focus more of my time, energy, and resources into those. I protect my heart by placing all the people in my life in their appropriate category. I realize some friendships and relationships are for a season and others are for a lifetime. Without being resentful, I understand that just because certain people are around me doesn't mean they are in my corner. They may not necessarily be against me, but they are not necessarily for me, either. I accept this truth and continue to be great without feeling guilty for leaving certain friendships of the past, in my past. I am still cordial and positive towards these individuals, but I no longer feel the need to fake a bond that has ceased to exist. I am liberated to pour into people who pour into me. I am free to not worry about how I am perceived by people who have not consistently demonstrated the love and positivity they say they have for me. Without any bitterness in my heart, I forgive them and I forgive myself for over-investing in friendships and relationships that have yielded bad fruit or no fruit at all. I don't let this impact the relationships in my life that bear good fruit. Rather, I cultivate the soil around those relationships so they continue to thrive.

Kelli took a picture of this SOI when she finished reading it. She knew this one belonged to her.

Donovan locked onto a SOI that was between two golden swords with crimson red hilts, located at the front of the combat zone. He felt chills as he read it.

Laziness and procrastination are my mortal enemies. Everyday I wake up, I fight against them with my entire being. I will not be fooled into thinking I have time to put-off the important things in my life. Time waits for no one. I am an executor and I get shit done. I am efficient and effective, actively working toward every one of my goals until they become an undeniable reality. I make the ideas in my head tangible through discipline, focus, and a clear plan. Therefore my success has longevity. On the days when laziness or procrastination get the best of me, I brush it off and get back into the fight the next day. I win more than I lose to these enemies. I allow my mind and body the time they need to rest. This is strategic and purposeful. I do not let myself get seduced by laziness, I stick my spear right into its heart. I take procrastination by its greasy scalp and cut its head off. Laziness and procrastination mean to rob me of my purpose and the mark I'm destined to leave on this earth. Everyday, I get up and go to war with disbelief, the enemy that makes me susceptible to laziness and procrastination. I release heat-seeking missiles of faith and confidence that obliterate disbelief. I have the power to carry out my dreams, desires, and goals. Nothing can hold me back!

Donovan yelled out, "That's what the fuck I'm talking bout!" catching the attention of a few nearby gladiators who gave him a nod of agreement.

Leilani didn't know what Donovan had read that got him so fired up, but she was close by when she saw and heard him yell. She saw the exchange between him and the other gladiators, too. This made her even more energized to find her SOI. She walked over to the opposite side of the combat zone, hoping to find similar inspiration. Then, she found it.

My life is coming together in perfect alignment. I don't have to be anxious about anything, I don't have to force anything. Things are happening as they should, even if it doesn't seem like it at the time. I can rest in that I am putting forth my best effort even if the outcome isn't what I want. I don't have to solve every problem or be the solution to every issue. I do what I can without sacrificing my wellbeing and mental health. I have trust that the people around me will figure out the things they need to without me having to do their work for them. Sometimes, mistakes will be made and balls will be dropped, but that's ok. This puts other people in a position to pick up the slack and realize more of their capability. I am at peace and rest, letting go of the clutter and excessive noise in my life. I focus on what is most important. I give my precious time to the causes and people who mean the most to me. I no longer fall into the trap of trying to gain acceptance by being everything to everyone. I'm cool with me, I accept me, I love me. By fully embracing this truth, I am able to better love and accept others for who they are. I have narrowed my focus and set my intention toward only doing things that make my heart leap. I have created a beautiful life I passionately manage. I have my shit together and I am at peace.

Leilani sat down on the floor near this SOI and let the words soak into her mind. She reread them again and again.

A few moments later, Philip announced, "Alright everybody, time is up for picking your SOIs. Let's come back together in the boardgame area. I hope you all were able to find a SOI that deeply resonates with you. And if you weren't, I am confident that based on the ones you saw, you can write your own. These are words that you will carry with you for as long as you need them. Then you will create new SOIs for new situations and circumstances you face."

Everybody sat down at the Gladiator Game™ tables in eager anticipation.

"Ok, let us continue the next part of our journey," said Philip. "Before we crack open these games, though, does anyone have any questions?"

# ACKNOWLEDGEMENTS

This book was literally written through my blood, sweat, and tears. And I am so grateful to be able to share a piece of my journey with you and I hope it empowers you to be fearless in the pursuit of realizing your fullest potential.

I am absolutely nothing without my Heavenly Father and His Son, Yeshua the Christ. It has been my faith in Him that has allowed me to weather every storm and to become the gladiator-King I am today.

My source of inspiration, Phil Jr., a.k.a. Lil Sharp, and Jonathan Jacobs, a.k.a. Baby Sharp, you are my WHY behind virtually everything I do and my pursuit of being the best man I possibly can, in order to be a strong and solid example of masculinity and what it means to be a conqueror in life. I love you with every ounce of my being.

My mother, Bishop Gwen Coates, thank you for your unconditional love, cheering for me, and always speaking my name in the rooms you are in. I love and honor you.

My sister, Lanicia, thank you for always having my back through the good and the bad. Thank you for always going to bat for me. Wink wink. I love you!

To my creative partners at Blue Cactus Press, Chris and Knic, we did it again! Thank you for helping me bring another one of my wild-ass ideas into the world. You are truly the best team I've ever worked with. After we breathe a little, it will soon be time for the next project! Love you both!

# ABOUT THE AUTHOR

Philip "Sharp Skills" Jacobs is a modern-day Renaissance man. He is a creative visionary, legacy builder, and cultural force reshaping the future in real time. An award-winning hip-hop artist with a message and a mission, he's also the creator of *Reveal the Elephant*, the groundbreaking racial equity board game, and the founder of *Fades & Finance*, a financial education platform empowering barbers and stylists to build wealth beyond the chair.

As the CEO of *Rebel Firm*, Sharp Skills fuses entrepreneurship, artistry, and social impact to challenge systems and uplift communities. A proud graduate of Seattle Pacific University, he was honored with the prestigious *Medallion Award* for distinguished alumni.

He is the author of five transformative books:

*Gladiator: Modern Parables for Building Resilience and Mental Toughness*

- *Accuracy: A Guide to Living Skillfully and Successfully in Today's Crazy Times*
- *You Are the Solution: Awakening the Entrepreneurial Spirit Within*
- *Quincy's Life: Daddy's Gone*
- *Elephant in the Room: A Modern-Day Parable About Race and Equity Conversations in the Workplace*

Originally from Inglewood, California, Sharp Skills now calls Spanaway, Washington, home. From there, he continues to inspire others while raising his two greatest legacies: Prince Philip Jr. and Prince Jonathan.

# ABOUT REBEL FIRM

**G**o against the grain of what a corrupted world system tells us to be by daring to reach our full, God-given potential."

This is the mission of Rebel Firm. It was birthed in the mind and heart of founder and CEO Philip "Sharp Skills" Jacobs during class when he was a community college student in 2003. That mission of growing and unleashing rebels on the world is as real today as it was more than two decades ago.

Rebel Firm is a Heroically Creative Consultancy and Production Company with four key areas of expertise:

- Success + Leadership Motivation Communication
- Music Production
- Book Publishing
- Racial Equity Consulting

Rebel Firm exists to equip rebellious leaders to

**Be Bold. Stand Out. Pursue Purpose. And Not Fold.**

We do this through 1:1 consulting/coaching, speaking engagements, workshops, panels, music performances, books, and other various forms of content.

*Gladiator: Modern Parables for Building Resilience & Mental Toughness*
by Philip "Sharp Skills" Jacobs

This book is a work of fiction. The story and characters are fictitious. Certain long-standing institutions, agencies, groups, and historical events are mentioned, but the characters involved are wholly imaginary.

Book packaging by Blue Cactus Press
Cover design and layout by knic pfost

Rebel Firm Books | Spanaway, WA